Cryptocurrencies and Blockchain in the 2020-2030 Decade:

How to Ride the Wave of Bitcoin, Altcoins and Decentralized Finance while Investing even a Little Money

Dexter Wade & Flavio Simeri

INTRODUCTION

I have made this work in such a way that the reader can use it in two different ways:

The first way is to open the text at random and read a single chapter or paragraph at your leisure since the topics, although they have a logical sequence, are not bound to each other.

This way it's like flipping through a magazine where you choose the article that interests you the most.

The second way is to read the text from beginning to end.

This will take you on a little journey into the way of cryptocurrencies.

Whatever your choice of how you want to use these pages, it will still be fine as long as you can understand it and apply it in its entirety.

Happy reading.

IS BITCOIN REALLY SIMILAR TO COPPER?

According to the Head of Commodities Research at Goldman Sachs (Jeff Currie who has also been head of CNBC), Bitcoin and cryptocurrencies would not be an alternative to gold but to copper.

Currie therefore speaks out on both digital cryptocurrencies and Bitcoins, but we will need to bring attention more to the latter because only Bitcoin is deflationary in nature and has a fixed, guaranteed and predictable monetary policy, while the other cryptocurrencies do not.

It can be said that everything revolves around the concept of **hedging against inflation,** so it is understood to be hedging against inflation risks.

To clarify this limitation, it is necessary to focus on the definition of **inflation**:

> Inflation occurs as prices rise, this is directly proportional to the decrease in purchasing power of money, obviously with the same amount of money.

When there are particular risks of inflation, the first action of investors, particularly those who have a large amount of money at their disposal, is to "hedge", in a certain way "get rid" *of* money to buy **assets** that do not lose value, unlike money.

However, as Jeff Currie points out, there are two types of inflation:

- **Good** Inflation - this generally consists of the price increase, which is generated by a growth in demand for the product (more people want to spend and therefore the price is increased to increase the gain on demand);

- **Bad** inflation - this is the exact opposite of good inflation, as it is generated by a shortage of supply as a result of which the price increases.

These two types of inflation are completely different from each other, in fact, while so-called bad inflation casts a pessimistic light on the future due to rising prices and low production, good inflation is paradoxically good in reality, because it implies that consumers are willing to spend their money and thus generates an optimistic light on the future.

Currie points out that when the scenario is **pessimistic, investors** tend to prefer to invest in safer assets, also called **risk off** which literally means "low risk."

It is also true that risk off assets lose less, which means that in a disadvantageous situation, it will be better to invest in this way, buying gold for example, because you gain little, but you lose less.

This would be the case if the money was simply left in the checking account to lose purchasing power due to bad inflation.

The scenario of good inflation is different, where investors cannot be as happy since, as explained above, it is true that the investment risk is lower, but it also generally allows for lower gains.

They therefore prefer to opt for **risk-on** investments, i.e. high risk, usually associated with commodities such as **copper** and **oil.**

To talk about Bitcoin, this currency is certainly not in the risk-off category, it is not a safe investment; therefore, we will say that **Bitcoin is risk-on**.

Although it is a hedge against inflation, it does not resemble gold at all since it is not a low-risk inflation hedge, therefore suitable for pessimistic times when inflation is bad.

In contrast, Bitcoin fits the hedge for risk-on, high-risk inflation, as it can potentially give those who invest or use it, higher returns in a good inflation scenario and you therefore have an optimistic outlook.

If one shifts the focus to the US market, for example, in the scenario for April 2021, particularly for consumer goods, inflation increased by 3.1% compared to the previous year.

In fact, in May 2021 it exceeded 4%, so it was at a time when there was strong inflation in the US.

Statistically comparing the monthly price trend of Bitcoin with that of gold over the aforementioned period, it can be observed that:

- The price of Bitcoin has fallen;

- The price of gold has increased.

Currie draws simple conclusions from these statistics: just during the month of April, when the strong US inflation took place, the latter could be considered bad, as it was due to a supply shortage caused mostly by the lockdown period for Covid-19 but also due to the low production and the shortage of raw material that guarantees the market.

Investors readily took refuge in investing in gold rather than Bitcoin because, as explained earlier, inflation being bad they needed to protect themselves from the risks that come along with it.

That's why they use a risk-off hedge like gold.

Comparing instead, in the same scenario exposed above, the price of copper with that of Bitcoin, we can observe that:

- The price of Bitcoin has fallen;

- The price of copper has declined, despite the fact that it was increasing in the period prior to the lockdown.

The lowest price peak for both categories compared was between May 19 and 20, 2021.

Subsequently, the prices of both (copper and Bitcoin), rose again towards the end of May 2021.

So it can be inferred that in recent months the price of Bitcoin has been more similar to the price of copper than it has been to the price of gold, therefore more like an asset that serves as a hedge against inflation but risk on, i.e. copper and less like the risk off of gold.

Although the U.S. is still experiencing bad inflation, there is a belief that the market will recover thanks, perhaps, to an increase in demand due to an excess of dollars created and put into the market.

The timing of a possible recovery is not easy to calculate but it is clear that inflation will become good, there will be an increase in demand followed by an increase in price.

MAXIMUMS AND MINIMUMS

Analyzing Bitcoin's time series since 2013, i.e., since we started receiving all the data day by day, we can see that, almost always, the annual **lows** or **highs** are *touched* at the **end of the year**:

- In 2013, the peak of the Bitcoin price occurred on November 30, thus at the end of that month, continuing on that figure roughly until December of the same year;

- The following year, in 2014, Bitcoin's lowest price occurred on October 5, so again near the end of the year;
- In 2015, Bitcoin's highest price occurred on November 4;
- In 2016, Bitcoin's highest price occurred on December 9;
- In 2017, Bitcoin's highest price occurred on December 17;
- In 2018, Bitcoin's lowest peak occurred on December 15
- In 2019, the only exception, Bitcoin's lowest peak occurred on June 26;
- In 2020, Bitcoin's highest price occurred on December 31.

In 5 out of 8 cases, the year ended with a peak, whether minimum or maximum, but always in the last months of the year.

In 3 out of 8 cases, the maximum peak occurred in December, the very final month, while in 2 out of 8 cases there was a minimum peak, also in the December period.

Framing this statistic more from above, it can be inferred that in 7 **out of 8 cases**, with the exception of the year 2013, the lowest or highest peak occurred at the end of the year.

It is fair to ask why this trend is occurring, and to understand it, one must align with the following hypothesis:

> First, you have to start by taking into account taxation, as large investors and traders pay **taxes on any capital gains.**

Note that capital gains are recognized only when you sell, so if at the end of the year you were about to sell, waiting until the beginning of the following year to sell you could **move the arrival of capital gains** and therefore taxes to be paid on it to the following year.

So at the end of the year, those who are making big gains might have an incentive to wait to sell, so as to reduce the pressure to sell Bitcoin when prices are particularly high.

The same discourse is worth, vice versa, if it arrives to the **end of the year with of the minusvalences**; it is convenient to sell endured in order to use them in order to reduce the taxes since these are not only paid on the plusvalences but on the difference between plusvalenza and minusvalenza.

Therefore, if you arrive at the end of the year with a low price, it is better to sell now and not wait until the beginning of next year so that you can discount any capital losses in the current year.

So, it's not at all a coincidence that at the end of the year when **prices** are **high,** there tends to be a peak, therefore the highest price of the year, because the **selling pressure tends to reduce**.

Conversely, in years that end with a very **low pri ce, there is a** tendency to note precisely the lower price because **selling pressure increases**.

It would not be surprising if, at the end of the year 2021, the maximum price occurs, i.e. exactly as it did at the year 2013 which was preceded by a continuous bull run in the previous year (2012).

Likewise happened for 2017 after 2016.

In both years mentioned the maximum price occurred at the end of the year between November and December, so we will have to wait until the end of 2021 to be able to say for sure.

Similarly, one could look to next year, 2022, at the end of which the annual minimum price could occur instead, again around December for example.

The year that was an exception was 2019 (when the highest price occurred in the middle of it in June), and it was such thanks to **Facebook**'s announcement that it was developing **stablecoin libra**.

So there was an anomaly that completely changed the annual outlook, but in every other year from 2013 to the current year (the 2021), there were price lows and highs in the last months of the year.

There is no total certainty that the situation will repeat itself this year but it is (as explained above), a valid possibility given the history.

BITCOIN IN THE WORLD

There are currently approximately 7,800,000,000 people on planet Earth but there are only 18,700,000 Bitcoins in the world, it is easy to deduce that in other words this means that there are not enough Bitcoins for everyone.

However, one must consider that each Bitcoin is fractionable into 100,000,000 parts, so **the smallest fraction recordable** on the Bitcoin **blockchain** is $\frac{1}{100000000}$ of Bitcoin, and is referred to in the jargon as **Satoshi.**

Since for each of the 18,700,000 Bitcoins in the world there are 100,000,000 Satoshi in circulation, this means that their multiplication will result in the **world of Satoshi** or **1.87 million billion.**

Looking at this number, one understands that if there are not enough Bitcoins for everyone, there are definitely Satoshi's for everyone.

If you divide 1.87 million billion Satoshi by 7.8 billion people, you get that, on average, there are **240 thousand Satoshi for every person** on earth.

To date, a single Bitcoin is worth **57 thousand dollars** and dividing this number by 100,000,000 you get the number of Satoshi that corresponds to it, then multiplying it by the 24 thousand Satoshi owned on average by a person, you will get **$ 137**, or even how much owns on average each inhabitant of the earth in Bitcoin.

Obviously, not the entire population owns it, but only a small portion of it.

Multiplying 137 dollars by 7.8 billion people results in about 1,068,600,000,000 dollars which is, precisely, the total capitalization of the Bitcoin market.

If we then multiply the latter number by 1.2, we get the dollar amount of 1070,000,000,000, i.e. the same capitalization described before but in a different currency.

The number of people who actually own Bitcoin, since it has been seen that the vast majority actually do not, is between 100,000,000 and 200,000,000 out of 7.8 billion people.

Two clarifications need to be made about the calculations that have been performed:

- The value of Bitcoins that has been used is that of May 12, 2021, but this value can change, so much so that these calculations could already be redone in a few months, and certainly in a few years, and give completely different results;

- The number of 18.7 million Bitcoins in circulation is a theoretical number, because in reality a portion of them are lost, as if they exist but cannot be used.

This was not done on purpose but is the result of an unintentional error, it would be a few million, but the fact remains that 18.7 million is still a bogus number as it lacks the subtraction of lost Bitcoins.

In other words, the numbers used above are approximated by excess, but approximating them by default we could say that on average each inhabitant of the earth owns about 100 dollars in Bitcoin.

These numbers serve to understand the level to which the value of Bitcoin has reached overall.

IS IT POSSIBLE THAT ONE DAY BITCOIN WILL BE WORTH 1 MILLION DOLLARS?

"Can 1 bitcoin be worth 1 million dollars?"

Although it seems like a trivial question, the answer is much more complex than it may appear.

If Bitcoin ever manages to reach the 1 million dollar figure, the question must be asked whether it will reach this number in today's dollar currency or that of the future.

This simply means that 1 million dollars will always remain so, but its true value is not its nominal value, but what you can buy with this amount.

It is certain that the value of 1 million dollars will be markedly different between today and a time period of 10, 20, 50 or 100, and different even between these periods themselves.

Traditional currencies such as the dollar, tend to lose value over time in fact, going into the future, we will observe again a decreasing purchasing power.

So a spontaneous but logical question arises:

> If Bitcoin were to grow to be worth a million dollars, what would be the purchasing power of this money?

As of today, we cannot know either when a Bitcoin will be worth a million dollars or what the presumed purchasing power for it will be.

The answer, therefore, remains very complex compared to the question, which is variously trivial, it is a simple hypothesis that makes us think on many fronts since there is no certainty but only opens doubts.

Bitcoin was created to be a deflationary currency, therefore to increase its value over time, while the traditional currencies such as the dollar mentioned above were created as inflationary currencies therefore destined to lose their value over time, if they were to begin to lose a lot of value over time and inflation were to be particularly high, the Bitcoin would have better chances of reaching the fateful threshold of one million dollars.

Note well that, if this hypothesis were to arise one day, it would be important to remember that it is true, a Bitcoin will be worth one million dollars but its purchasing power will definitely be less than the million dollars today since, precisely, it has lost its value over time contributing to the opposite rise of the Bitcoin currency.

In order to compare the value of Bitcoin with its true purchasing power, one would have to use a price expressed in another currency but with what one can buy with a Bitcoin.

Making this comparison is reasonable if you relate it, as mentioned above, within 10 years of the present, because going too far back in time, perhaps 50 years, does not even allow you to know what products will be on the market and at what value they will be sold.

The same reasoning could have been made by anyone born in the 70s who could not predict what products would be on the market in 2020 because they are totally different from that era.

So, a Bitcoin in the future is more likely to achieve a dollar exchange rate of 1 to 1 million than it is to achieve the purchasing power of the value of 1 million dollars.

Unfortunately, there is still no tool that measures the real purchasing power of a Bitcoin without having to associate it with its exchange rate in dollars or other currencies yet.

Another legitimate question to address on this topic is whether (given all the parameters argued above), ***Bitcoin will really manage to get to be worth a million dollars or not***, clearly referring to a single Bitcoin, not to the total value of all Bitcoins that are in circulation, since to date all those circulating are worth more than a trillion dollars.

So, we will have to focus on the value of the single Bitcoin in question, so it will be useful to remember that every single Bitcoin in turn can be divided into 100 million parts and 1 millionth of Bitcoin, or its smallest part, represents 1 Satoshi.

As of today, 1 Satoshi is worth a thousandth of a dollar.

To answer this doubt, we need to consider 2 graphs showing respectively:

- **BTC / USD** (meaning **value of Bitcoin in U.S. dollars**), in this chart the first important thing you notice are the major growths that occurred in 2016 and 2021, when it went from $1,000 to $20,000 and then from $20,000 to almost $60,000.

So, it is clear that this currency has this potential for very rapid growth.

If instead of focusing on what will happen in the next few months and years, you would focus on what will happen in the next few decades then you will notice that instead of making these **big rises in value**, Bitcoin might even be able to reach the 1 million dollar mark.

Since the target market for Bitcoin is the U.S. market, it is appropriate to consider the $1 million in dollars to get a true sense of the exchange rate.

- **STOCK TO FLOW** which is the logarithmic chart where the price of Bitcoin is expressed from $0, then $5, then $10 and so on until the price it has reached to date.

The graph features a big red line that represents the **direction** that the value of Bitcoin is chasing, so whether it is increasing or decreasing.

For example, by the end of 2021 it could reach $100,000 and by the end of 2025 it is supposed to reach $1 million.

However, this information is only assumptions based on past parameters and does not represent a rule but simply a projection of what would happen if the past trend were to recur.

It is absolutely necessary to distinguish very carefully the two expressions "**could do it**" and "**is likely to do it**" because they look similar but hide a big difference.

In fact Bitcoin could as well as could not reach the million dollar mark.

But the important thing is not whether or not it can reach it, the important thing is how likely this thing is to happen.

To date, no one is able to say with certainty what are the chances that the price of Bitcoin will sooner or later really reach one million dollars, so the hypothesis that it may succeed in reaching this value and the hypothesis that it does not are to be considered almost equal.

In this reasoning everything fits until we have to reckon with inflation, which, as has been said before, contributes voluminously to the loss of purchasing power of the American dollar.

The greater the loss of purchasing power of the dollar, the greater the increase in the price of Bitcoin will be.

So the greater the inflations on the dollar, the greater the likelihood that Bitcoin will one day be worth $1 million.

If this probability were reversed and therefore if the probability of the dollar not decreasing in value due to inflation, it would mean that the probability of Bitcoin reaching $1 million would also be significantly lower.

In conclusion, it is important to understand that asking today if Bitcoin will come to be worth this amount tomorrow is still too premature because you cannot have any kind of certainty or probability, since what is possible is also impossible.

What makes the difference is trying to calculate according to past trends the probability of them happening again.

BITCOIN: DEFINITION

There is a big difference between **bitcoin** and **Bitcoin**, as the lowercase letter indicates the protocol and instead the capital letter indicates the financial asset, i.e. the actual coins.

Defining the protocol is unfortunately still complicated, but instead as far as the financial asset is concerned, there has been a response from the head of the section of Goldman Sachs that deals with research on commodities, i.e. raw materials.

His name is Jeff Currie and in an interview he explained how Bitcoin's asset can be considered as risk on, or high risk investment.

There are assets that are facilitated by the **hedge** fund and, therefore, you protect yourself from the risks that you may have when you invest in them.

In fact, Bitcoin is an asset that has this, as when you invest in Bitcoin you are protected from inflation.

However, it remains a high-risk investment because it is very volatile and tends to change price very quickly.

However, there are also currencies such as gold that protect against inflation but are low investment risk.

Currie's definition has been very successful, not only in the financial markets but also among Bitcoin users who have shown a lot of acceptance for his words.

Of course, all of this is nowhere near enough to say with confidence that this is the definitive definition, but it does give a very clear and very likely idea of what it might be. Also because it tends to be the case that the other alternatives for defining it have not been commonly accepted, while Currie's is widely accepted.

High-risk inflation hedging means that people who own money, usually in large amounts, at certain times are afraid that this money will lose value due to inflation, which sometimes increases and sometimes decreases.

This happens because currency can lose purchasing power, so if its nominal value essentially does not change, what can be bought with that currency changes

Another way to hedge against inflation is to invest in **gold**, which is **risk off**, although at critical times it often loses some value.

It is an investment that could allow for low losses but low gains.

If you want to take a risk instead, you can invest in Bitcoin, waiting for its value to increase significantly in hopes of making a profit.

Great wealth managers don't just have dollars, gold or Bitcoin, they own all three to really be facilitated.

They are, however, accountable to banks for their financial accounts.

So this is the role that Bitcoin is quite clearly carving out for itself within the financial system, and if things go on like this, it will become increasingly **clear** and **stronger** what role it precisely wants to play in this world system, not least because we are in a time of decreasing inflation and therefore increasing purchasing power of traditional currencies.

WHAT DETERMINES THE VALUE OF BITCOIN?

The value of Bitcoin is determined solely and exclusively by the relationship between supply and demand on the markets on which it is traded, however while this statement may seem simple, in reality, the scenario is quite complex.

First of all, its value is nothing more than its market value, i.e. how much you can get if you sell it on the market (even if we tend to take the exchange rate in US dollars as a reference point).

So, when you say for example that Bitcoin is at 9 thousand dollars, it means that the exchange rate between Bitcoin and dollars is precisely 9,000 to one, that is, you need 9 thousand dollars to buy 1 Bitcoin.

Therefore, the exchange rate at which that last trade took place, is referred to as the price of Bitcoin, which is why it varies all the time, in fact these exchanges happen all the time and always at different prices.

But the point is that each platform, and each Exchange, use as a reference point the last transaction that took place on the same platform and therefore for each platform there is a different price because the exchange rate at which the last exchange took place on that platform is certainly different from that at which the last exchange took place on another platform.

The price of Bitcoin is shown on average as the price that is given on the Exchanges, but of course there are those who sell it for more and those who sell it for less.

It tends to vary so much because the supply must also adjust to the number of requests.

Generally, it works in such a way that if demand increases, the price of supply also increases, and vice versa, if demand decreases, supply in the markets also decreases.

In moments of stability between supply and demand, it does not mean that Bitcoin are not being traded, certainly it is done with less volume but we are always talking about tens of thousands of dollars. If the demand were to increase a lot, the supply would tend to remain stable, but as always this detail cannot be established beforehand because the price of Bitcoin is constantly fluctuating.

When the collapse of the financial markets happened, supply skyrocketed, so to speak. Everyone was going to sell Bitcoin, as a result the price collapsed while instead, during the last big speculative bubble at the end of 2017, demand increased enormously which made the price increase tremendously in no time.

Over time the price then fell back, precisely because it had been fueled by the speculative bubble.

It's good to remember that supply and demand can basically do 3 things: grow, stay constant or decrease.

The causes that can move the price in the marketplace are many, and the sum of all of them then tends to set that price.

It is such a complicated dynamic that it is often impossible to identify a single and unique factor that has moved the price of Bitcoin, first and foremost because the price of Bitcoin moves through supply and demand.

Both, in turn, are due to multiple causes so it is very difficult to draw a conclusion on who has influenced more and who less in the change in price, demand and supply (except, for example, when an important item was involved, such as Facebook making statements in 2019 about new technologies, and at the time of the rise in the price of Bitcoin, it was already known to whom to attribute the causes, although not all because, as mentioned above, the factors that contribute to the variation are many).

Over the years, the value of Bitcoin has practically always increased.

This happened precisely because it was designed to be a deflationary currency, as opposed to the classic traditional currencies such as the dollar.

In an article on Bitcoin.news, a table was published showing the price of Bitcoin as of 2013.

The average price was $249 and then in 2014 it was $521, and so on.

In 2014, it increased 110% over the previous year, and then decreased again by 48% in 2015.

Then, in 2016, its value went back up 109% and its average value remained at $564.

In 2017, its average value came in at $3,900, an increase of 592% from the year before.

In 2018, the average value was 9,000 with a 105% increase from the previous year.

This sequence of yearly changes demonstrates that Bitcoin is truly a deflationary currency, as its value has increased significantly despite short falls such as those in 2015, which have largely recovered.

It was created to continue to gain value over time, but that doesn't take away from the fact that you may experience price declines as well.

There is no certainty that it will always increase but it is properly designed for that to be the case, barring unforeseen events, which, however, do not depend on supply since the number of Bitcoins that are minted and distributed is fixed.

The hypothesis is that Bitcoin is a deflationary currency, that is, a currency that continues to increase in value over time, since nine years after its creation, thanks to this data and the time series that have been seen, this hypothesis seems to be confirmed.

UNDER WHAT CIRCUMSTANCES IS BITCOIN WORTH MORE?

Bitcoins are not all the same, in fact some have a history and some do not.

The latter, which have no history, are called virgins and are more valuable because there is a specific market demand for them which are, by the way, very few.

Virgin Bitcoins are those that have a clean transaction history or even no transaction history at all.

All Bitcoin transactions are recorded on the Blockchain which is public, so you can go and check and trace the entire history of all transactions in which a particular Bitcoin or Satoshi was involved.

You can go and check when it was created (as of today, 12.5 Bitcoins are created every 10 minutes or so) and then follow all of its various movements from one address to another.

Some of these movements are the result of illegal activities and are kept under control by the authorities and sometimes Bitcoins that come from these activities can even be blocked or confiscated.

There is no problem if Bitcoin is used as it was intended i.e. peer to peer, person to person.

An Exchange is an intermediary in which to change Bitcoins into dollars and dollars into Bitcoins; these Exchanges are, generally, regulated or at least should be and therefore subject to the anti-money laundering rules that are imposed by the states.

This means that these state-recognized and regulated intermediaries can step in to seize any Bitcoins that come from illicit activity, or they can even reject them.

There are, however, precisely some Bitcoins that either have no history or have an absolutely clean transaction history.

Those that do not have a history, are those newly minted and never used, those that have been created on the address of the miner who used to mine the block and always remain there; they are the so-called virgin Bitcoins that have no history and have never belonged to any transaction. They were created put on the address and that's it.

There are also others, always defined as virgins, which have an absolutely clean transaction history, but are usable and have not been lost.

Those that have an absolutely clean transaction history are very few.

Most have a history, they have been part of multiple transactions but there is no certainty that these transactions are clean so there are precisely dirty Bitcoins as well.

It is very difficult for an ordinary person to be able to go and check all the transactions in which Bitcoin has been involved, or in which Satoshi has been involved.

So, to cut to the chase, there are some people looking for transactional-free bitcoins.

Certainly, there are very few cleaners and this makes there is a specific market demand for these virgin Bitcoins and they have a higher value than the others (estimated to be between 10% and 30%).

Who has the possibility to have clean Bitcoins on his address, therefore with no transactions, or with very few transactions definitely clean, has in his hand Bitcoins that are worth a bit more and could find buyers willing to pay more.

It is no coincidence that the greater value of these virgin Bitcoins is very small.

By the way, in the future it is thought that there will be more and more registered on the public Blockchain, so you can't even call it a problem because over time it should get smaller and smaller.

The value of these virgin Bitcoins might be decreasing rather than increasing also because 12.5 of them are continuously generated every 10 minutes.

Those who mine Bitcoin use the rewards that come with it to make transactions and use everything right away however, perhaps, a portion could start not using it and register it on their address and then, perhaps, resell it at a higher price to those who need virgin Bitcoins.

The technology of Bitcoins is really complex and different than what you are used to in the past and compared to the old fiat currencies.

In the old fiat coins, there are virgin dollars and gold, which are all the same.

There are some transactions that are followed by law enforcement because they are the result of illegal activities however on the market, if you find virgin dollars, for example cash, they are traceable so all dollar cash bills have this feature that instead Bitcoin does not have, since there are banknotes.

All transactions are tracked when new Bitcoins are created and thus a new issue arises i.e. a new small parallel market of these Bitcoins that have never been used or have only been used for clean transactions and thus are considered clean in turn.

BITCOIN: SINGLE CURRENCY

Bitcoin is a special, indeed absolutely unique, currency.

A coin like this had never been created before.

What makes it so are two characteristics: decentralization and a deflationary nature.

In 2009 (when it was born), Bitcoin was the first currency in the entire history of mankind to be decentralized, in fact it makes use of the peer-to-peer network, also called peer-to-peer.

Already from the name you can deduce its definition, that is the parity between all members and therefore between all nodes that are in the network.

This means that there is no one to change the characteristics of Bitcoin or what is issued from it.

Completely different is the situation for traditional currencies that are subject to the management of central banks, which can decide how much money to issue on the market or eventually withdraw them from circulation.

In fact, what distinguishes Bitcoin is that it is self-controlled thanks to the computer protocol it has, which is a list of operating rules that must be followed to the letter, otherwise the node is automatically excluded from the network.

This protocol could, in theory, mutate but to do so, almost all Bitcoin users would have to agree to stop using old Bitcoin protocols and switch to new ones.

This is a very difficult assumption to assess.

The other important feature of Bitcoin is its deflationary nature which is opposed to the inflationary nature of fiat currencies.

To fully understand what the difference is, it is necessary to know that the European Central Bank annually maintains a 2% rate of inflation, that is, an increase in product prices and a decrease in the purchasing power of money.

These last two sentences explain what inflation is and why it is a means of making money for banks.

But the deflationary nature of Bitcoin is that if you have a bunch of money and you set it aside, it won't be affected by inflation for two reasons: the first is that it's not managed by the bank so the 2% rate doesn't apply to them, and the second is that Bitcoin is a currency designed to increase in value over time; given the limited amount of Bitcoin that will be in circulation, it can't be devalued in the same way as fiat currencies.

Many banks, such as those in Venezuela for example, have unfortunately encouraged the rise in inflation to the point where the local currency (the bolivar), was withdrawn because it was no longer worth anything.

Obviously, it's good to reiterate that you can't predict how the value of the Bitcoin price will change, but since the protocol has proven to be designed precisely so that it will increase over time (with lots of practical tests), this is a more than plausible hypothesis.

In fact, an example with which you can clearly see the difference in the effects of inflation on fiat currency and what happens instead thanks to the Bitcoin protocol is that if you put savings aside, those in dollars, for example, lose purchasing power over time, while those in Bitcoin have a high probability that they will acquire it.

In fact, it would seem that Bitcoin is great for reserving and traditional currency is instead great for handling trade, as its purchasing power could easily be lost over time.

HOW TO INVEST IN BITCOIN

Investing in Bitcoin is equivalent to buying Bitcoins by paying in dollars, so it basically means doing a currency exchange from dollars to Bitcoins.

This works similarly to when changing from dollars to foreign currencies such as the euro, British pound or Swiss franc.

To change dollars into Bitcoin there are special sites called, not surprisingly, Exchange wich allow you to deposit your own dollars and, with these, to subsequently buy Bitcoin from other users who are doing the opposite, that is, they are selling Bitcoin to acquire dollars.

Since Bitcoin is precisely a currency, it is fair to ask: *How do you make money by investing in a currency?*

You simply try to buy Bitcoins at an affordable price to maybe resell them tomorrow at a higher price.

This usually happens with traditional fiat currencies like the pound, but it does not happen, or at least happens very rarely, that dollars are bought (for example) to be resold later at a higher price.

For Bitcoin it's the exact opposite because it has essentially an opposite nature to fiat currencies that are made to lose value over time; Bitcoin currency was made to gain value over time so tomorrow it will probably be worth more and buying it now could mean reselling it in the future at a higher price.

It is not said, as already explained, that this happens with certainty but there are probabilities.

Making an investment in Bitcoin is by no means just about winning, it's a high-risk investment like others and can have bad results too, not just gains.

Therefore, you have to be especially careful of those who promise assured gains with investments in this currency, as it is not predictable but only depends on the prices with which you were able to buy and subsequently sell the Bitcoin currency in dollars.

From a practical point of view, you have to start by signing up in some of the Exchange sites where after depositing the dollars, you can use them to buy Bitcoin.

The only major difficulty may arise at registration, where the procedures that rightly follow the requirements of the law are long and drawn-out.

Exchanges can be distinguished into:

- Simple, which are convenient for anyone who wants to make use of them but don't allow you to do all the tasks that a professional would do.

- Complete, which are more lent for professionals.

Generally, you start with the simpler ones and progress to the more comprehensive ones over time.

It is advisable to be registered on several Exchanges and not choose just one, the reason is very simple because these sites every time go offline and do not allow the use, therefore, it is obviously better to have more than one on these occasions, always remembering that the registration process is long and it is convenient to make these registrations first in several Exchanges so as to have more accounts available at the time of need.

- **Binance** - is most likely the largest crypto exchange in the world and contains a huge number of cryptocurrencies while the three Italians listed above have few.

It's a very comprehensive but equally complex tool, so to get started, it's best to register to get an overview of how it works, but keep it as a backup site until you're more familiar or experienced;

- **Kraken** - another excellent site which, as explained above, it is advisable to register and use only after practicing;
- **Coin base** - born as an entry level Exchange, so to make small transactions and has developed as a great platform, although it is slightly surpassed by others such as Conio and Binance for the high costs and the support service only in English and not very efficient.

Once registered in the Exchange sites you have to deposit dollars in the accounts and then use them to make Bitcoin purchases.

It is not recommended to buy Bitcoin by credit card because the costs are very high, the best solution is to pay by bank transfer considering that nowadays many banking services offer the transfer at zero interest rate, so completely free.

Having explained how to buy, it is also good to say when and at what price to buy Bitcoin.

To earn money it is obviously appropriate to buy them at a good price to be able to resell them tomorrow at a higher price, so you have to find this good price.

It tends to be better to buy when the price goes down and sell when the price goes up; however, many users use another method of investing which is the so-called **accumulation plan** or **pack**, in a nutshell they make several purchases of little value from time to time at the end of the month.

This way, you're always buying at a different price and reducing the risk of buying at sky-high prices.

Typically, this process takes place continuously for a long time until you have set aside a good amount of Bitcoin.

Afterwards, you stop there and store the accumulated Bitcoins in your wallet until you need them, without having to wait to figure out when it's best to sell them instead.

If money is needed tomorrow, then that may be the opportunity to resell it.

Accumulation plans are done directly on the trading sites, moreover some banking services also allow you to schedule transfers to the Exchanges and schedule Bitcoin purchases later on the Exchange sites according to your preference and need.

To recap:

- Investing in Bitcoins is equivalent to buying them when they are low priced and selling them when they are high priced;

- If you don't want to wait for price changes, you can do an accumulation plan with timed purchases to reduce the risk of buying at high prices;
- Do not store Bitcoins on the Exchange site but move them on your wallet because, as already mentioned, sites tend to stop working from time to time maybe for various updates, but the money on the wallet

are always active and ready to sell. It's good to know that for example Conio doesn't work only from Exchange but also from wallet.

- To earn money you have to sell Bitcoins by moving them from the wallet where they were deposited to the Exchange, then you will collect a sum in dollars that you can withdraw from the site.

HOW TO EARN MONEY BY INVESTING IN BITCOIN?

In theory, investing in Bitcoin may seem easy but it is a complex process that can very likely lead to loss rather than gain, especially when you are a novice.

It is very important, therefore, to have proper training on the subject, study and practice before you start investing large sums.

There are several ways to earn with Bitcoin but the most popular one that we will discuss below is also the one that may seem the most trivial.

It mainly consists of buying Bitcoin at a low price to resell it when it has a higher price.

These selling and buying prices are made by the market, and in order to take advantage of them you have to choose the perfect time to buy and the even more right time to resell.

But the right time is extremely difficult to guarantee because no one knows for sure how the price of Bitcoin will vary over time; it's just a matter of probability.

So there is always a certain probability that the price may increase and a certain probability that it may decrease.

Of course, as with all trades, professionals who trade on a daily basis more or less know how to estimate the probability of Bitcoin's price.

But, those who are beginners, will have a hard time and it is good to train and gain experience one step at a time because otherwise they risk working following only their intuition and making mistakes.

It is good to rely on competent people for these analyses.

It's not enough, however, to be able to calculate the probability of the best time to sell, you must also try to understand how quickly these price changes occur.

It's also easy to lose patience because it can take days as well as it can take years for the price to go back up.

If, for example, you know that the price within 30 days could go down, then it's a great time to invest and earn maybe in two weeks a 30%.

But neither the price change nor the timing of the change should be taken for granted.

It is convenient to be enrolled in an Exchange to carry out these buying and selling operations because in these sites the dollars are deposited, therefore the investments and from here they will be ready for purchase as soon as the perfect moment comes.

After the purchase, always on the Exchange, you can make the sale and here you will have to wait for someone to want to buy your Bitcoins.

If it doesn't happen in the immediate term, there is no need to worry because it can easily happen in the future.

But you also need to be well informed about these exchange sites, as they may have peculiarities such as perhaps selecting only one type of currency pair rather than another, and this could put the seller in trouble if they do not have any at the time of the proposed sale to the market.

To recap, there is no guarantee of making money in Bitcoin, and you don't have it especially if you don't evaluate the risks outlined above.

IT IS POSSIBLE TO CREATE DOLLARS THANKS TO BITCOIN

You can use Bitcoins to create dollars out of thin air.

It is actually a cryptocurrency token that has the exact same value as the dollar and is therefore like the actual dollar.

This is called **DAI** and its value is precisely one dollar.

If you look at its history, you can see the way its value always fluctuates around that of the dollar, so there will be days when its price will be slightly higher or lower, but it will always be around the same figure.

This is because it is artificially held around this value.

These tokens made specifically to keep the value around that of the dollar are technically loans:

Cryptocurrencies are taken and immobilized within a smart contract, which, in turn, creates DAIs that the user will use at will.

Obviously, since it is a loan, there are fees to pay and sooner or later you have to pay them back, otherwise the smart contract after the collateral (i.e. the guarantee), will no longer be sufficient will sell it automatically and the user will no longer be the owner of the guarantee remaining only with the DAI that had been granted in exchange for it.

On the other hand, if you wanted to recover the cryptocurrencies that had been put up as collateral, all you would have to do is return the borrowed DAIs and pay the interest on the loan itself.

To date, 131,794,831 DAIs have been created, which corresponds concretely to about the same number of dollars in circulation.

In other words, there are 131 million dollars that have been created out of nothing and that are added to the dollars already in circulation but, in their smart contracts, are immobilized (and therefore unusable), of the collateral consisting of Bitcoin and other cryptocurrencies.

In this case, we are not talking about a stablecoin like the USDT, which unlike DAIs does not add money supply to dollars because on the one hand it subtracts it and immobilizes it, on the other hand it issues it.

Instead, as far as DAIs are concerned, the only coincidence with the dollar is, precisely, the value which is almost the same but does not increase the dollar money supply, rather, it immobilizes other cryptocurrencies and, later, issues them as US dollars from a token that has the same value as the dollars.

This technology of creating dollars from Bitcoins is used to spend cryptocurrencies without having to worry about volatility and without having to sell them, because when Bitcoins are immobilized by the user on the smart contract to create DAI, in reality, only the user can withdraw them and can only do so by returning the loan.

This did not sell the cryptocurrencies but provided the opportunity to use them to have a loan of similar US dollars that you could spend.

This operation is risky because, if the value of Bitcoin decreases, the user in question will still have to give back the DAI and interest from the loan to get back their cryptocurrencies, which, at that moment, might even be worth less.

Since this is completely decentralized and legal, it is an unstoppable process, and the only drawback that can happen to the user is the loss of their currency due to non-payment of interest or failure to return the DAIs they borrowed.

Since it is not a token that represents American dollars but a token that simply maintains its value similar to that of American dollars in an artificial way, any doubt about the legality of this process can be safely erased, as the dollar currency is not in any way interpolated and is only and solely used as a reference point.

WHY YOU SHOULD BUY BITCOIN

The choice to buy Bitcoins is completely free and arbitrary, it is obviously not mandatory in any way to own them.

The right question to ask about this topic would be "how do *you benefit from buying Bitcoin?*"

The reasons could be grouped in three examples, but before doing so, it is appropriate to remember that those who buy Bitcoin are subject to the various risks explained above and therefore must do so in the midst of their free choice:

1. **The speculative reason:** if you believe that over the next period the value of Bitcoin might increase, then it would be optimal to buy Bitcoins in order to resell them at the time of the price increase.

Also here you have to take the risk of loss in case the price of Bitcoin does not increase and therefore it is not possible to sell it at a higher price than the one at which it was purchased.

There is no certainty in this reasoning, you can not know for sure what turn the price of Bitcoin will take but you can just *speculate*.

1. **Bitcoin's deflationary nature** - Traditional fiat currencies such as the U.S. dollar and even the euro have, unlike Bitcoin, an inflationary nature, so they lose value over time.

The Certal banks have a commitment to **inflate** these coins by about **2% per year**, which may suggest that perhaps in 12 years they will lose little value but in decades they will lose a lot of value.

A **great example** to illustrate this hypothesis might be the following:

Suppose that 1,000 dollars are deposited in a personal current account, if there was an average inflation of 2% every year, in 10 years these 1,000 dollars would have the same purchasing power as 817 dollars even though it would still be 1,000 dollars.

After 20 years, their value would drop to 668 dollars and after 30 to 545 dollars.

In other words, at a constant rate of inflation of 2% per year, €1,000 today will be worth about half that in 30 years.

Bitcoin was therefore created to be a currency of a deflationary nature, that is, it should do the opposite and accumulate value over time by increasing its price.

This has already happened, in fact if you look at the price of Bitcoin on a large time scale, in the years 2009/10 the price of Bitcoin was significantly lower than it is now.

By the way, the current inflation rate of the Bitcoin money supply is, in fact, about 2%; in 4 years it will drop below 1%, in another 4 years it will drop below 0.5%, and so on until, by 2030, the inflation rate of the Bitcoin money supply will have dropped so low as to be irrelevant.

All this means that Bitcoin will not suffer from money supply inflation in the long run.

This, in theory, would bring the price in time and in years to increase more and more. Obviously there is no certainty that this will happen, we simply speculate on past events that seem to repeat their course, therefore in the future events of this type could re-consolidate.

A very good way to exploit this example is to understand that money, euro or dollars, if they remain stationary in the bank will lose value, after a long time, but still they will lose it, so it is convenient to convert a part of it in Bitcoin, leaving it on the wallet and hoping that it will gain value.

Again, as before, you take a risk, as Bitcoins may not gain as much value as you hoped in the wait time from purchase to sale.

1. **Financial freedom** - is a motivation in itself that can be said to be particularly different from the previous two, because if you want to make transfers in dollar (i.e. fiat currency), in large quantities, especially abroad, you will come up against limitations. There are even countries where if you send dollars you receive the money in the local currency already changed, while for Bitcoin, as for many other cryptocurrencies, there are no limitations of any kind or other types of obstacles to run into because the Bitcoins can be used in any amount you want to do it.

There are cryptocurrency tokens on the market that have the same value as fiat currencies which are known as stablecoins in technical jargon.

The best known and famous is the Tether or USDT which has the value of the US dollar.

These currencies allow you to make free transactions without any obstacles or limits around the world in a cryptocurrency token that has the same value as fiat currency.

Again, as before, it is worth reiterating the risk you take when buying Bitcoin.

Buying Bitcoins and storing them with care is relatively simple but not very easy and the same reasoning should be applied to any type of operation concerning the use of Bitcoins because they all require accuracy, precision and above all a lot of attention, so you should be cautious and well informed from the beginning about the risks and all the rules to follow.

ARE THERE ENOUGH BITCOINS FOR EVERYONE?

Within the Bitcoin protocol it is clearly written that **no more than 21 million Bitcoins can ever exist.**

Clearly, the Earth's population consists of over 7 billion, almost 8, people, which is almost 300 times more than Bitcoin's 21 million.

The question that arises is "*are there enough Bitcoins for everyone or will only a few people own them?*".

Bitcoin's limitation, as mentioned earlier, is that there can never mathematically be more than 21 million people in the world who own more than 1 Bitcoin.

However, a Bitcoin is divisible into 100 million parts, similar to the dollar which is divisible into cents but into many more parts which are called Satoshi.

This means that for every Bitcoin there are 100 million Satoshi; if you multiply the 21 million Bitcoins by the 100 million Satoshi, you get 2.1 million billion Satoshi.

As a result of this calculation, we can see that now the population is not so much bigger to share the Satoshi to everyone.

Satoshi and Bitcoin are the same currency expressed differently; a plausible and well-known example might be the kilogram compared to the gram, which express the same thing in two different units.

In other words, whoever owns Bitcoin also owns Satoshi and whoever owns Satoshi also owns Bitcoin; if for example you own 2 Bitcoins, at the same time you own 200 million Satoshi because they are the same thing expressed with a different unit of measure.

Therefore, the fact that there will never be more than 21 million Bitcoins in the world will never be an issue as Satoshi would be used instead of Bitcoins which in terms of meaning are the same thing.

There will be no distribution issues for Satoshi.

Another interesting comparison that can explain the situation taken into account is that between Bitcoin and dollars, but not in terms of the number of Bitcoins in circulation compared to the number of dollars; rather, it is appropriate to look at Satoshi in comparison to cents since dollars, in general, are fractionated into cents even if, if desired, they could be fractionated further.

As far as dollars are concerned, there are a few thousand billion in circulation at the moment; in all likelihood, there are tens of trillions.

Clearly, to find out the number of cents in circulation, you have to multiply the number of dollars by 100 and the result is that the number of cents in circulation in the world is about one million billion.

As for the number of Satoshi in circulation, however, it is, as mentioned above, 2.1 million billion.

Certainly, an exact comparison cannot be made since the total number of Bitcoins that will be able to circulate has not yet been reached (to date, 18,470,593 Bitcoins have been created, which corresponds to 1.8 million billion Satoshi).

The amount of pennies present today is comparable to the amount of Satoshi.

No one has probably ever wondered if there are enough pennies in the world, because the answer is trivially that, yes, there are enough pennies.

And, since their number is perfectly comparable to that of Satoshi, it is clear that there are also enough Bitcoins for everyone.

HOW MUCH IS IT POSSIBLE TO EARN WITH BITCOIN?

Actually, the question in full would be "*how much money do you make investing in Bitcoin*?"

Since Bitcoin is a currency and there are many ways to earn Bitcoin, for example you could do a job and get paid in Bitcoin.

Referring to investments in Bitcoin, it is true that you can but you have to be very careful because Bitcoin is considered **a high-risk asset**, which means that there is also the possibility of losing everything.

Often inexperienced investors who invest in Bitcoin end up losing, for this reason first you should know Bitcoin and become a little bit experienced to be able to then invest in these assets because if you invest without being an expert, it is very likely that you will not only not gain but even lose.

Also, since it is precisely a high-risk asset you have to be careful because those who promise significant gains from investing in Bitcoin without then saying that there is also a high risk of losing, are lying.

Therefore, it is good to stay away from all those who promise great gains in Bitcoin without saying that in reality this is an investment that might not only not necessarily bring gains, but even lose money.

You can't predict the gains from investing in Bitcoin that you will have when you are able to buy Bitcoin at a low price and sell it back at a high price, much the same way you do with stocks on the stock exchange.

The logic is pretty much the same, but the problem is that it's extremely difficult to know when the price of Bitcoin is low or about to rise, and it's also impossible to know for sure what the price of Bitcoin will do in the future since it could go up, it could go down, or it could even stay put.

So, a person who invests in Bitcoin randomly has a two out of three chance of not making a profit because, if the price drops you don't make money rather you lose.

If the price remains stationary, you don't make money and therefore you only make money if the price has increased.

> The highest price ever reached by Bitcoin is about $62,900 and was reached in April of the year 2021 due to a speculative bubble.
>
> Previously, there was another speculative bubble in 2013 that led to a previous spike in December 2013 and then again in December 2017.
>
> In fact, if someone had bought Bitcoin in December 2013 at $1,000, so during the first big speculative bubble, and sold it in December 2017 at $20,000, during the second big speculative bubble, they would have sold at 20 times that price.

So if, for example, you had invested 100 dollars in December 2013, then in December 2017, (four years later), you would have sold the same amount of Bitcoin you bought with 100 dollars for 2,000 dollars.

By buying in July 2015, when the price dropped to $250, you could have resold in December 2017 at the peak of $20,000 (80 times the initial price, i.e., the purchase price).

Therefore, investing 100 dollars in July 2015 to December 2017 by selling Bitcoins you could have cashed in 8 thousand dollars.

It is possible that there could be other bubbles in the coming years that could generate even greater gains.

However, it is almost impossible to imagine that Bitcoin from now on will allow you to multiply your invested capital by a hundred.

In fact, the further you go with time, the more these huge gains shrink so it's hard to imagine that you can multiply your money by 80 in the future.

These reasoning made in hindsight, seem very simple instead, having to face the future and having to decide now whether to buy or not, when to buy and how much to buy, in anticipation of what may happen in the future everything changes completely because it is impossible to date to know where the price of Bitcoin will go.

Before asking yourself these questions, it's good to first try to understand what Bitcoin is, understand how the price evolves and then maybe make certain choices like risking investing in Bitcoin with the possibility of losing it or maybe gaining something.

ARE BITCOINS LEGAL?

Bitcoins are absolutely legal (although there are countries in the world that have declared cryptocurrencies illegal, such as Nepal and Bolivia).

In other countries, however, such as China and Japan, there is no law against using them.

There is published Resolution 72 of 2016 from the Internal Revenue Service, which legally explains how you need to deal with cryptocurrencies regarding, for example, taxation policies.

Often, the fact that there is no law on cryptocurrencies simply indicates that they have been integrated either to the principles governing foreign currencies or, more easily, they are allowed to be used without problems.

As far as Bitcoin companies are concerned, with the currency decree they must be considered as foreign currencies, therefore the same rules are followed as with dollar transactions, for example.

Taxes, in fact, are paid on all transactions made in cryptocurrencies and on any capital gains because, at the end of the year, you have to necessarily declare in the budget how many of these currencies you own with an exchange rate in dollars.

You'll need to make a budget that starts in dollars and ends in dollars but, in the meantime, you'll use converted cryptocurrencies.

For private individuals there is a threshold of possession below which, these transactions in cryptocurrencies, are not taxed because the Italian state, actually just the revenue agency, in that resolution considers these currencies as if they were foreign currencies and therefore they will have to be declared in the balance only when they will be brought to the standard currency (the dollar).

The minimum limit that is set is 51,000 dollars, so if you have more it is good to be followed by an accountant.

Investments in cryptocurrencies are considered high risk, this means that you have to be very cautious in making them since, if you invest in a currency in a completely uninformed way, you risk losing all the money you invested.

It would be wise to invest what you are willing even to lose.

Investments are a gamble in time that is certainly not worth making for those who have little patience because it can take years for a currency to change its value.

That's why it's a good idea to carefully inform yourself about the coins you want to invest in, use objective data and try to make a prediction of the price in the future.

For some information and techniques, it is suggested to use Bitcoin.news as a source, where market analysis and numerous trading strategies are published so you can improve your skills.

To trade it is good to start with investments you are not too fond of because, as mentioned before, you could lose money.

The holder often buys devalued cryptocurrencies and even holds them for many years until the price goes back up, so they can sell them back and make a profit.

The trader buys to resell, possibly in a short period, and tries to take advantage of the ups and downs of the market because his main interest is to create a capital gain or an income in very short periods.

However, trading is a risky business and done by professionals;

For beginners, the best thing would be to buy tokens on Exchange sites and start from there to practice step by step to learn how these currency exchanges work.

They could also use platforms that make use of CFDs, similar to tokens, for continuous trading.

If you buy tokens, it's a good idea to store them in your wallet until you want to sell them again or trade them.

There, too, you can observe whether their value goes down or up.

It is also possible to do the opposite process, i.e. sell tokens and acquire currency that you can then either reinvest or use at your leisure.

The trader holder, instead, is the one who holds (as exemplified before), his own cryptocurrency for a long period of time carrying, so to speak, a lot of patience until a price change.

These are not very complicated processes, you just need to learn how to make purchases and moves, but these small operations have nothing to do with real trading which is an extremely precise and delicate trade.

Traders, for example, work on the Kraken platform, which is very hostile in use.

Another impressive platform is Big Stamp which, however, does not allow you to convert cryptocurrencies back into dollars, rather, it always has them reused in the purchase of cryptocurrencies.

But the most popular one is definitely Binance.

Yet another one is Cex.Io which is a platform unfortunately of dubious management, but it works very well and admits a lot of cryptocurrency types in exchanges.

These platforms are not all for novices, therefore, it is reiterated that one must be cautious and informed when investing money and using the Exchanges.

To get started, you can sign up for all the best and performing ones.

IS BITCOIN REALLY A BETTER CURRENCY THAN GOLD?

Bitcoin is often compared to gold because it is seen as a possible store of value, but in reality Bitcoin is better than gold in some respects.

Business Insider published the tweet of an inquiry made by a journalist who went to a number of stores in New York to make purchases and ask if she could pay with gold bars or with Bitcoin (the gold bar has a value of about 4 thousand dollars).

It turned out that no one agreed to pay with gold bars basically for two reasons:

- No one trusted it because they couldn't know if that bar was really pure gold;
- They could not weigh it and quantify its value to see if it was worth about $4,000.

While instead some retailers have accepted payment in Bitcoin.

The journalist showed that in New York, if you want, in some places you can pay with Bitcoin, while virtually nowhere you can pay with gold.

On the other hand, when someone wants to make a payment in Bitcoin, you do not need any kind of trust, because Bitcoins are not in any way falsifiable so, if you receive Bitcoins, you are sure to have received a certain precise amount of Bitcoins, not one more and not one less. They are all definitely real, while with gold there is always the problem of fakes, because you do not know if that bar is really gold and if not it is perhaps only partially.

You don't even know if the weight is correct and you really should weigh it on a scale.

The value of gold is certainly less volatile than the value of Bitcoin, which is still volatile as well, but the value of gold in the market varies much less over time than the value of Bitcoin, which varies as much and as fast.

The conclusion reached by the journalist is another, namely that no one doubts the fact that gold is a store of value even if, nowadays, it is not a transactional currency and is not used as a medium of exchange.

Even Bitcoin tomorrow, if it were not to be used widely and extensively as a trading or transactional currency, would actually probably still continue to remain a store of value.

It's still a bit of a stretch to define Bitcoin as a store of value, however, it's safe to say that that's its primary intended use and if it truly delivers on all the promises (so if it holds its value over time) then it will be used as a store of value.

As an alternative to gold, there is the advantage that to spend it you have to practically sell it and then cash fiat currency and spend it.

On the other hand, as far as Bitcoin is concerned, it can always be cashed out of fiat currency and spent, but in some cases it can also be used by spending it directly without having to change it into fiat currency.

Gold is not a currency with a deflationary nature so, generally, it is not convenient to spend it but to keep it and probably it will never be used as a medium of exchange or as a transactional currency at the same level of fiat currencies; in fact, probably, people will continue to use mainly euros and dollars.

Paradoxically, it seems even better but, in reality, it's at greater risk; the beauty of gold is that if you physically own a gold bar you will own it forever, it won't disappear between one thing and another.

Bitcoin has a higher level of risk than gold but is so much more convenient and so much easier to use that it could probably even, in certain contexts, take the place of gold as a store of value.

That is, if it truly proves that it is deflationary in nature and therefore maintains, or even increases, its value over time.

There are also cryptocurrencies called stablecoins pegged to the value of gold that symbolize it, as if they were certificates of ownership of physical gold (which is actually kept inside a vault).

It can be said that cryptocurrencies have solved the problem of the difficulty of exchanging gold because, if instead of exchanging physical gold, you exchange cryptocurrency tokens with the exact same value as gold, you can practically even use gold as you do with transactional coins.

That being said, the big difference between Bitcoin and gold remains, which is value stability.

The value of gold is relatively stable, it is not fixed, it varies and changes over time although very slowly.

While the value of Bitcoin is much more volatile and that really appeals to traders, that is, those who make investments and trades in the market to try to make money.

Traders in fact, hardly make trades on gold, which varies little, but they make them more likely on stablecoin currencies because they vary a lot and they can earn a lot more.

Bitcoin, having higher volatility is therefore more suitable for buying and selling (trading), speculation and exchanges; while gold, on the other hand, is more suitable for long-term storage.

Inflationary currencies, such as fiat currencies, will most likely remain the main means of exchange precisely because they are inflationary (as long as inflation is not exaggerated, which must always be controlled at around 2%).

But, until then, they will likely continue to be used as trading currencies.

CAN BITCOIN DROP BELOW THE LOWS AND GO BELOW ZERO?

It is possible, in theory, that the price of Bitcoin will return to 0, which is exactly where it was when it was created in January 2009 (more than 10 years ago).

But this is very unlikely to happen.

The fact that it is possible has nothing to do with the fact that it can actually happen, on the contrary, it is so unlikely to happen that it can be said that it is an option completely to be neglected and left out since it is irrelevant at present.

Looking at the logarithmic scale graph of Bitcoin's price trend from the beginning until today, we see that in the beginning it was 0 and has been for a year and a half, then it started to rise first towards 0.1, then towards 1, then towards 10, and again towards 100 and 1,000.

It then went back up and went over 10,000 in late December 2007 and then came back down.

You can see from this chart that it is very difficult to imagine it going back to zero from here.

The graph (which you can find on the internet by simply typing in "Bitcoin graph" on Google) shows the price trend to make it clear that the current trend is shown to be increasing and never triggered a downward trend that will take it down to zero but has simply oscillated over time.

So while it's entirely possible that Bitcoin could even go back to having 0 value like it did in the beginning, it's also extremely unlikely, so much so that it's not worth considering as a realistic option.

Also the dollar, in theory, could go to 0 (like any other fiat currency, like the Zimbabwe dollar that went to 0. In fact at some point its real value, not its nominal value, thus its purchasing power, was completely depleted. So much so that on April 12, 2019 it was withdrawn from the market since it was no longer worth anything).

Even fiat currencies can run the risk of going to zero as an effective value and disappearing but no one believes that the dollar can go to 0, while instead fiat currencies, as demonstrated by the Zimbabwe dollar, can go to 0 so much so that they are even withdrawn from the market.

Fiat currencies can be destroyed by inflation and brought to 0 value but for Bitcoin, hyperinflation cannot exist because the issuance of new Bitcoins is regulated and fixed, and too many Bitcoins can never be issued.

It is already up to 18.5 million Bitcoins issued, and the maximum is 21 million, so very few will be issued.

Instead, in the case of fiat currency where the issue is left to the central bank, it can issue as many as it wants.

These are the assumptions that make it extremely unlikely that Bitcoin can go back to zero, as well as the fact that the dollar can go to 0; in fact, it is so difficult that you have to consider it a purely theoretical assumption.

All we know for now is that Bitcoin is very volatile, so it can also go down a lot and up just as quickly.

THE DEFLATIONARY NATURE OF BITCOIN

Bitcoin, from a financial point of view, is an asset that has a very unique feature: its deflationary monetary policy, therefore it opposes inflation.

Inflation is the increase in prices over time and the devaluation of currency that is often caused by the issuance of too much money on the market that ends up making it of little value.

The process of inflation is driven by central banks, such as the ECB, the central bank of Europe or the US Federal Reserve.

The banks create a lot of money and issue it on the market and the consequence is inflation.

In the history of mankind, there had never been a currency with an arbitrary policy that could not be changed or that did not have an inflationary nature, and therefore did not suffer inflation.

This is where Bitcoin comes in, which was born with a deflationary nature, decided from the start never to be changed in any way again.

Bitcoins are distributed every 10 minutes, that is, after the last block of the blockchain has been inserted, and a precise number is distributed that is decided by its own protocol. This number is halved every year because there is a limit to which the number of Bitcoins will reach and, after which, no more will be issued.

This date is around the year 2140. Whereas for fiat currencies an inflation rate, a price increase rate, of 2% each year must be maintained.

Bitcoin is characterized by the *locking of* a private key, so whoever is in possession of Bitcoin but loses the private key for some reason, will no longer be able to use it from their wallet, which is where they are stored.

The moment Bitcoins are no longer created, but can only be lost, will be the moment when the currency will truly show itself to be deflationary despite the fact that, over time, it has already shown itself to be so on numerous occasions.

This will not depend on inflation, because it is not managed by banks that instead apply money supply increases to fiat currencies.

Bitcoin was created just like a currency that, however, does not have to undergo devaluation at the hands of banks, it must be completely autonomous from them and depend on the supply and demand of its market.

When no more Bitcoins are produced, there will be a reversal and its deflationary nature will begin to be more noticeable.

If you look at the history of the US dollar fiat currency, you can see how it has lost a lot of purchasing power over time.

The opposite happens for Bitcoin, which has done nothing but increase over time.

Even if the demand for Bitcoin were to remain stable in the future (because precisely no more will be produced), it would still increase its value since it depends not only on demand but also on supply.

Certainly to be able to say with certainty that the nature of Bitcoin is as it has been described so far, we have to wait patiently.

Obviously no one has the power to change it or modify it, but anything can happen perhaps for financial reasons over time.

The only world in which it can never, ever be changed is the virtual one, that is, in its protocol of use.

For all the reasons listed up to this point Bitcoin is considered better than many other cryptocurrencies on the market with a deflationary nature, because it is a financial instrument that allows, at least so far, to fight inflation.

IS IT POSSIBLE THAT BITCOIN WILL ONE DAY DISAPPEAR?

The news that mining Bitcoin is no longer worthwhile is actually incorrect.

This is the news published in the newspaper "il Sole 24 ore" and someone could think that, if it is no longer convenient to mine Bitcoin, then it could die together with the mining of itself, that is together with the mining that is the operation necessary to carry out the transactions.

So if there is no one undermining Bitcoin, does *the system cease to work*?

It's not happening and it won't happen.

To understand why, we must start from the assumption that mining is no longer convenient. First of all, the minimg is an activity full of costs (higher than revenues), in a nutshell, who mines it at a loss, not earning but losing money.

In fact, mining actually allows Bitcoin to be mined which can then be sold on the market, specifically at market price; but this activity also has significant costs because a lot of electricity is consumed so if the costs are greater than the revenues, *why would anyone mine Bitcoin*?

The hypothesis could be that no one wants to mine Bitcoin anymore since mining is essential but without mining there are no transactions i.e. Bitcoin.

So this news may seem true but is totally false for two reasons:

- Although the price of Bitcoin is more or less the same around the world, this does not apply to the costs.

In fact, the main cost, that of electricity, varies because it costs very differently in different states.

There are still states like Venezuela, where the cost of electricity is so low that mining Bitcoin is still a more than profitable activity.

So you don't then need to have so many miners around the world for Bitcoin to work, if you mine where it suits you, the consumption is relatively less and there is a greater prospect of profit.

> So, for example, if the US, Italy, Germany or Japan were to stop mining Bitcoin, maybe instead in China there will be someone who will continue to mine; so it will be enough that there is someone who continues to mine and Bitcoin will go on.
>
> For this reason, it will be very difficult for the price to fall below the minimum cost.

It's good to remember, however, that if the price of Bitcoin goes up, the cost of mining tends to go up as well, and conversely, when the price of Bitcoin goes down, so does the cost of mining.

Bitcoin was created so that things work in a simple way.

- The market value can rise or fall very quickly while, on the other hand, the cost of mining rises or falls very slowly so, for example, at times like this, in several countries around the world the cost of mining is higher than the price of Bitcoin and we will have to wait a while because the process is not immediate but, if things stay like this, the cost of mining will automatically fall.

Mining is a competition in which there are many miners competing to mine blocks and then receive, in return, 12.5 Bitcoin as a prize for anyone who mines a block.

This competition is done with machines that have high computing power and try to find **cryptographic hashes**.

These machines consume electricity, and the more powerful they are, the more electricity they consume.

Over the years it is possible to reduce consumption with the same power but this does not happen in the short term, it only happens over the years.

So, if a lot of computing power is needed to mine Bitcoin, then inevitably there will be a high consumption of electricity which will obviously have an equally high cost.

In times like this, when the price of Bitcoin in the market is low, the risk is that this high cost due to high computing power is higher than the market price.

In fact, right now, some miners are shutting down their machines so they don't consume electricity because otherwise they would be mining at a loss.

That's exactly the point because the more the price goes down, the more some miners will be forced to shut down their machines to reduce consumption.

If someone turns off their machines because it doesn't suit them, others (i.e., those who didn't turn off their machines because it doesn't suit them), will make more money because competition will be reduced.

So, the more the price goes down, the more computing power that is committed to mining Bitcoins and the more it reduces costs for those who can still mine without losing out.

Those who turn off the machines will wait until the price of Bitcoin comes back up, but others, even if they are fewer, will continue to mine as long as it suits them.

It must be said, however, that the presence of miners who never turn off the machines, are a simple reflection of the fact that the system works well even if there are few miners.

Bitcoin was created so that even if you reduce the computing power, this in the long run does not impact the functioning of the system.

Specifically, there is a parameter called difficulty, which grows or decreases depending on how much computing power grows or decreases so as to make sure that on average the block is always mined every 10 minutes or so.

So the difficulty varies completely automatically, making sure that regardless of whether there is a lot of computing power or little computing power, Bitcoin will continue to be mined at the rate of one block every 10 minutes.

As of today, there is no danger that the low price of mining will cause Bitcoin to disappear because it doesn't pay off and there won't be in the future either; these adjustments are automatic, albeit slow, because the price varies very quickly but the changes in hash power, i.e., computing power and difficulty, are a bit slower.

WHY WILL MANY CRYPTOCURRENCIES DISAPPEAR?

Something similar to what happened with **TCP/IP** could happen with Bitcoin in the next 50 years.

When the internet was created, they were looking for a protocol to use for communications within it and, between the 70s and 80s, there was a real war of protocols from which only one emerged victorious, **TCP/IP**.

There were lots of other protocols still in 1990 that were then pretty much abandoned.

There is a hypothesis that something like this could happen to Bitcoin because, if you don't think of Bitcoin as a financial asset or a computer technology, but look at it as a protocol (which it is), it is not impossible that one day it will establish itself as the basis of the whole crypto system and that it will be basically the only one.

Then again, Bitcoin nowadays already has two uniquenesses:

- Its market capitalization which is greater than the sum of all other cryptocurrencies (so the market is split with half of Bitcoin);

- Stable coin is already being developed, there are already so-called Bitcoin layers such as lighting network which are additional second layers that have been introduced and are based on the Bitcoin protocol.

The internet also works in the exact same way, for example the web is at a higher level with http, with html, with client server and with browsers because trivially the **TCP/IP** protocol allows all server computers connected to the internet to communicate with each other.

So, if the evolution of the Bitcoin protocol were to follow the same fate as the evolution that followed TCP/IP, in a few years, or a few decades perhaps, we will find ourselves having a lot of higher layers developed on Bitcoin and having the latter as the only basic standard, or at least as a standard used by a lot of systems.

In fact, the only real digital gold is Bitcoin and, in theory, other protocols can be developed on other cryptocurrencies as well.

Among cryptocurrencies and tokens, there are more than 2,000 in circulation that are based on third-party platforms, such as all the tokens that are based on Ethereum; in the future, there may be a lot of them and they may be released on the market but, if we focus on cryptocurrencies, i.e. platforms, protocols and blockchains, it must be said that actually not everyone uses them and it will be very difficult for at least 80 or more to survive.

It will initiate the so-called tokenization of the economy, consider that every company that has a stock that is traded on the market could be equipped with tokens.

Bitcoin with its deflationary nature is completely decentralized and has a very good chance of surviving and spreading even further in the future.

Then there are probably other similar protocols that will make room as well, but as it stands today, virtually all of the traffic that is on the Internet is based on using the TCP/IP protocol using these higher layers like apps (which are one such layer), or search engines for which the same type applies.

Something like this could happen, indeed easily will happen with Bitcoin: you will have Bitcoin as the standard protocol of use that will still leave little room for other protocols or other cryptocurrencies and blockchains.

Not all of them will disappear completely because there is to clarify that in some areas they are more performing but the moment you have many Bitcoin layers developed on the bulk of the cryptocurrency usage market will use Bitcoin.

So, in summary, on the one hand there is Bitcoin that could establish itself as a standard and occupy the large part of the cryptocurrency market thanks to second layers, i.e. protocols that are developed on top of the Bitcoin base protocol, on the other hand there is the fact that in the future it will be possible to issue tokens also on the Bitcoin blockchain and that there will be in place everywhere an organization of the economy, where tokens are exchanged through second layers based on Bitcoin.

There's one last thing to say: the other protocols for other blockchains that are going to do what Bitcoin does will most likely fail.

They will not be eliminated but their use will decrease dramatically.

There are many very interesting projects that are advancing, but the problem is that these platforms are many, it's a host of cryptocurrencies from which they will surely not all be able to emerge, maybe between 5% and 20%.

DEFI

The term **DeFi** refers to Decentralized Finance.

Decentralized Finance itself is made up of financial instruments that are not managed by individual entities but in principle by public IT protocols.

Public protocols are **smart contracts** that run on the blockchain (like Ethereum's) and can be found easily.

They indicate the programming code in plain text (which by reading you can also guess exactly how it is carried out) that is executed by the Ethereum virtual machine, which is precisely a decentralized network and therefore not controlled by anyone but simply based on a public **open source** protocol that runs on all Ethereum nodes, i.e. the computer on which a node is installed.

There are also other platforms besides this one that allow the execution of decentralized smart contracts, however Ethereum is the most widely used of them all.

The smart contracts on which decentralized finance is based are therefore nothing more than programs made from a code that is executed automatically by the nodes or software of the network, thus of the blockchain.

Therefore, they are not controlled or controllable by anyone since there can be input from outside that could be controlled by other people making the smart contract work in one way or another.

Typically the ones that are done best are those that either don't have input coming from the outside or, if they do, use so-called **decentralized oracles** that allow smart contracts to be sent with data from the outside.

These can be of various types between simple and complex, however, upstream, the operation is definitely complex.

However, you have to be careful as they are not always reliable or accurate; in fact, they have been around since the early days of 2018 so you are in the infancy of these new technologies.

Their tools were highly influential during the 2020s, you can all find and check them out on their "defipulse" site.

The dominant protocol at the moment is called AAVE and is worth about $1.5 billion, followed by MAKER with less than $1.5 billion and finally CURVE with $0.5 billion.

Those who want to use these protocols must necessarily deposit cryptocurrencies within the smart contract, and as long as this money remains within the smart contract, the user can use it; however, if they withdraw it, they cannot continue using the tool.

The volume of tokens immobilized within the protocols is expressed in U.S. dollars and gives an idea of which protocols have been most used of all.

For each of these protocols, you can see the downward or upward curvature.

This data is used to understand what the history of the protocols is and to express user trust because, if so many users wanted to lock tokens within a smart contract, one can imagine that it is commonly believed to be a more trusted protocol.

Instead, those who have convinced fewer people to deposit tokens perhaps have a lower level of trust.

It's good to remember that these platforms are very recent and often tend to fail in a short period of time (although you don't wish it), and risk taking away with them the tokens that users have deposited.

In addition, they are protocols that are momentarily out of reach for everyone but mostly bring profit to experts in the field.

To understand the work that protocols do, it is worth consulting DeFi's website because they are distinguished and categorized into **Lending Protocols, Decentralized Exchanges, Derivative Exchanges, Payment Instruments, and Assets**.

The most widely used are the lending protocols and they work as follows:

> If you have tokens, cryptocurrencies, on hand, you can immobilize them in one of these protocols that dispense loans and, in the meantime, you can borrow from another token.
>
> The classic case, for example, is to deposit Ether to borrow other stablecoin, another is to borrow these tokens to **trade on margin,** then with leverage that consists in betting on the price change of cryptocurrency using then, not only their own funds, but also those borrowed.

The latter is a very risky procedure.

Decentralized exchanges are sites where you can trade cryptocurrencies, buy and sell, and also trade.

They're not managed by anyone but smart contracting, though.

Let's take a look at some of the advantages of decentralized exchanges:

- In traditional Exchanges you have to hand over your tokens to the Exchange Manager, and if there are any problems, your tokens could be at risk of being lost forever.

The opposite happens with decentralized tokens since it is the direct owner of the tokens who always remains the owner and has exclusivity on his tokens.

Perhaps they may be lost in the trading process, but they cannot be lost at the hands of anyone other than the owner.

- Decentralized instruments could be found in any financial environment but they have one major limitation, which is that they can only exist and operate within the network system of the platform on which their respective smart contracts are uploaded.

So a smart contract on the Ethereum network can only run on this network.

This makes it very complicated to be able to use for example traditional currencies, fiat currencies, within the instruments of decentralized finance because they are not compatible.

The trick is to use tokens that represent fiat currency, the most famous, described above is the USDT that runs within the Ethereum network and can be used by smart contracts that run on Ethereum but, in reality, represents US dollars, for all intents and purposes contained in a bank account.

- Some of these protocols have their own token then issued, in fact, by the smart contract that perhaps, in recent months, has seen a significant increase in its value, one of these is **YFI.**

Decentralized finance is in fact in a moment of great growth and, consequently, there are some new instruments that are debuting in this market and are very successful.

Precisely because of the enormous expectations that support DeFi the *bursting of the bubble,* i.e. the fall in value, would mean a great risk for the entire platform.

It is therefore important to be careful with risks of this type and to know well the trend of these protocols before investing in them, and therefore not to buy at bubble prices, that is, too high, which could lose value in a short time.

DOES THE VALUE OF BITCOIN DEPEND ON THE COST OF MINING?

Bitcoin's market value, or its price, or exchange rate, in U.S. dollars does not depend on the cost of mining.

The price of Bitcoin is only given by the relationship between supply and demand therefore, if the cost of mining increases, the price of Bitcoin will not necessarily increase as well.

The chart that gives an idea of the trend of the mining cost and the chart of the dollar price compared show how the price of Bitcoin went up and then after that, as a result, the mining price went up, then at some point the price of Bitcoin started to go down and after practically almost a year the mining cost started to go down as well.

If the price of Bitcoin depended on the price of mining, the rise and fall of the latter's price would have happened before that of Bitcoin and it would not have behaved this way.

To date, the volume of all Bitcoins that have been traded is about 55,000; the price is driven by a very large volume of trades rather than the Bitcoins that are already in circulation and have already been mined, so the price of Bitcoin has not followed the cost of mining but vice versa.

In addition, the volume of Bitcoins that are mined and placed on the market is smaller than the total volumes traded.

Therefore, the price is not determined at the moment these mined Bitcoins are placed on the market because the market trades much larger volumes.

The market determines the price of Bitcoin independently of mining and mining costs but the opposite is true, i.e., mining costs follow Bitcoin price changes.

The moment the price goes up, since mining is a competition, it means that miners will be able to invest more and spend more on electricity to mine Bitcoin (because they are worth more if they take out other miners anyway).

When the price increases, as a result, although much more slowly, the cost of mining also increases because competition increases among miners who invest more when the price drops.

The exact opposite happens if the miners from these Bitcoins that they extract from the network make less money and are forced to reduce costs (otherwise they would go at a loss).

But the investment or a decrease in the investment of miners, always happens long after the growth or decrease in Bitcoin prices.

The Bitcoin network always works in the same way regardless of the cost of mining, i.e. if mining costs more or costs less, only 12.5 Bitcoins will always be issued every 10 minutes so that the predetermined number is always met.

Although they are issued every 10 minutes their value changes over time depending on the price, so miners to continue to earn are forced to adjust their costs to price changes.

Inevitably, the cost of mining goes up in order to increase investment and when the price goes down, miners are forced to shut down the machines to avoid making them produce at a loss.

In fact, mining consumes electricity at a very high cost.

BITCOIN MINING

Mining Bitcoin is absolutely not earning from nothing, in fact miners perform a whole other activity and they are not in the business of creating Bitcoins.

These are created by the management protocol which also determines how many it will create and how many it will distribute.

Bitcoins are released every 10 minutes, so after a new block is added to the blockchain.

The race to win the Bitcoins on the line is about finding the right cryptographic key that allows the last block to be concatenated to the new one.

This key must be found in 10 minutes, and it is done using competent and very powerful hardware.

Those who do so receive the sum of 12.5 Bitcoins in return.

This amount halves every 4 years since Bitcoin has, as per protocol, a fixed number of coins it leaves in circulation, after which it will not issue any more.

Those who do not have the necessary computing power will be at a great disadvantage when faced with other miners who may be using much more powerful computing software.

You might also be able to never undermine a block, but a somewhat supportive solution has been found, namely pools.

These are meetings of miners who share their computing power

Of course, this doesn't mean that once you enter a pool you will just win.

You must have your own equipment which must be compliant, powerful and punctually updated as the computing power required can be increased according to the difficulty with which the previous block was mined.

So it will be good to be equipped with all these materials to even hope to compete in computational power with other equipped miners.

Finally, the eventual receipts are divided and here we must reckon with the costs, since those who mine from Italy pay a very high cost of energy compared to those who do so from countries where it costs less.

This is a risk that can occur and if so you will make the miner work at a loss.

If you want to avoid the cost of equipment there is cloud mining.

Unfortunately, not everyone is honest and you can count reliable cloud miners on the fingers of your hand, as it is very easy to get scammed if you leave money to those who want you to believe they only want to help you earn money.

CAN YOU MINE BITCOIN FOR FREE?

Mining for free is absolutely not possible because Bitcoin mining has an electricity consumption cost.

Some solutions may be to mine from places where energy has a low cost or to self-produce it through a photovoltaic system.

The cost does not stop at the energy but to mine you need to have an excellent computational power and, to have it, it is important to invest in a good internal hardware, or buy an external one and take advantage of very powerful graphics cards

Obviously, this technology comes at a high cost given its power.

In fact, to mine Bitcoin, you can't just buy equipment bit by bit while you're doing it. It is good to have everything ready by making sure that all the equipment is correct and fully functional.

Another option, although debatable, is to make use of cloud mining, but the fact remains that free mining is impossible; you can only get back the expenses invested at the beginning in equipment and consumption, simply committing yourself to earn surplus value and cover these expenses.

WHY IS NO ONE SELLING BITCOIN WHEN THE PRICE GOES DOWN?

In a graph, very curious and very interesting, which concerns in particular the trading volume of Bitcoin during bull (price goes up) and bear (price goes down) periods, the interesting thing to note is the breakdown by cycles and therefore by periods; this shows that in the last cycle, at the end of 2018, the price touched new lows and after the all-time high of the end of 2017, during those moments when the price of Bitcoin went down, trading volumes were reduced to the minimum.

This chart shows these four cycles, each of which is identified by the minimum touched after the maximum.

For each of these four cycles, it shows the trading volume on days when the price went up and days when the price went down.

- During the first cycle (from 2010 until the end of 2011), the trading volume is quite sustained however there are also some nice trading volumes when the price dropped.

- In the second cycle (2012 through 2015), we can see that the trading volume when the price went up was significantly higher than the trading volume when the price of Bitcoin went down.
- In the third cycle (ended in 2018) there is a clear prevalence of trading as the price went up, while there is a decrease in trading volume when the price goes down.

The interesting thing is that in the clickloop from December 2018 until July 2009, the trade volume when price was going down is so small that it is not noticeable, i.e. in the last seven months the trades that took place on the Bitcoin blockchain were practically only on the days when price was going up, otherwise, on the days when price was going down the trade volume was minimal.

This can mean two things:

> In the last seven months, on the days when the price fell, there was very little Bitcoin traded, almost none.

> The cause would be related to the so-called **OTTs**, i.e., those who buy Bitcoins not to resell them, i.e., they change fiat currency into Bitcoins to keep them and no longer return to fiat currency, in other words, the vast majority of Bitcoin holders, when the price drops, do not sell.

This is a hypothesis that would seem to be supported by the previous data; after all, in the last seven months there has never been a resounding collapse of Bitcoin, therefore, a moment of panic in which everyone went to sell on the days when the price fell, because after the descent stopped, the price went back up. This happened most likely because there were very few people selling Bitcoin during that phase.

The reasoning can also apply in reverse, i.e. on the days when the price of Bitcoin has gone up, over the past seven months, the trading volume has been substantial.

A lot of Bitcoins were traded and on the day when the price fell instead, trades fell to a minimum.

In other words, it almost seemed as if no one wanted to sell Bitcoin on the days when the price was falling, and this probably could have triggered a halt to the fall in price during the falling days, precisely because of a lack of sellers.

An important clarification to make is that the data shown in this chart does not refer to Exchanges, but only to transactions on blockchain.

In fact, they do not take into account any transactions that may have taken place with lighting networks.

What is relevant is the fact that there are no transactions when the price goes down but there are many when the price goes up.

It would not be surprising in fact, every time an exchange takes place, there is someone who sends and someone who receives, someone who sells and someone who buys so here the volume we see is at the same time both buying and selling volume. The discriminant lies in the day in which these exchanges were made, that is on days when the price of Bitcoin went up because there were many people selling and buying, on the contrary on the day when Bitcoin went down there were very few people selling and buying.

HALVING OF BITCOIN

Halving means **halving** but when referring to Bitcoin it has another meaning.

It is, in fact, mining that serves on the one hand to validate transactions, but also to create new Bitcoins.

In fact, the miner who manages to mine a block, that is, to validate the block, is given a prize that consists of new Bitcoins that are just created within the block that was mined.

To understand the halving, all that needs to be said is that every time a block is mined, Bitcoins are created and given away to the miner who managed to mine that block.

The award that is given to the miner does not remain fixed forever.

When Satoshi created and started mining Bitcoin in 2009, the reward was 50 Bitcoins every time someone mined a block.

If you take into consideration that the new block is mined every 10 minutes, you can understand that 50 Bitcoins every 10 minutes over, say, a year is already a great amount.

But Satoshi had an idea: he made it so that **every four years this award would be halved**, and here's the halving.

This halving began in 2012 when there were only 25 Bitcoins being created in each block and then given away to the miner that mined it.

Then in 2016 there was a second halving that brought this figure to the current 12.5 Bitcoins, so as of 2019 12.5 Bitcoins are created every 10 minutes and given away to the miner who manages to validate a block.

The next halving occurred in May 2020 becoming 6.25 Bitcoin.

Around the beginning of 2024 it will become 3.125 and so on.

So over the years the amount of new Bitcoins that are generated decreases until at some point no more Bitcoins are created and no more rewards are distributed to miners.

There's no need to be afraid though because miners don't only earn from the premium but also from the fees.

Inflation of the circulating mass, i.e. the increase of coins in circulation tends to cause a reduction in prices while instead in Bitcoin this inflation is controlled, but decreasing over time until it runs out.

This is the so-called **deflationary nature of Bitcoin which** is then the opposite of the inflationary nature of traditional fiat currencies.

The idea behind Satoshi's reasoning is that if traditional fiat currencies lose purchasing power over time (they lose value precisely because of inflation), Bitcoin, on the other hand, should have a deflationary nature that could guarantee it the opposite, i.e., increased purchasing power over time.

Unfortunately there is a misunderstanding and often the term "inflation" is used to indicate the increase of prices and therefore the decrease of the purchasing power of money, but in reality originally referred to the increase of the circulating mass.

As of today, the inflation of Bitcoin's circulating mass is roughly 4%, so with the halving of May 2020, this inflation has dropped below 2%.

We're not talking about Bitcoin price inflation, but inflation of the circulating mass, i.e., the number of Bitcoins in circulation.

On the other hand, central banks' targeting of fiat currency inflation means the reduction in purchasing power due to rising prices, which is something however related to the topic but definitely different.

In 2024, Bitcoin money supply inflation will even drop below 1%.

It is a bit difficult to have certainties about how the price of Bitcoin will behave during the next few years however, it must be said that the reasoning to date seems to have proven to be correct.

There is no guarantee that it will continue in exactly the same way tomorrow.

BITCOIN AND EXCHANGES

Sometimes, when stock markets drop, so does the value of Bitcoin.

To explain this phenomenon we must start by looking at the trend over time of Bitcoin, therefore all the increases and decreases that describe its value, and compare them with those of the stock exchanges (S&P 500 the American stock standard).

It's good to have an overview of the years because you can clearly see how the two don't seem to be connected at all, in fact from the beginning of 2018 to now we find few and rare coincidences of movement, for the rest, they contradict each other.

This process is due to the issue of **liquidity** (the possession of cash).

On the financial market, in general, operators tend to use currency to buy financial assets (i.e. to invest) which they then in turn resell to re-cash the currency previously used.

This last coin is invested again.

In other words, the objective of financial market participants is to invest money, i.e. use liquidity, to purchase assets.

Based on this concept, when it is suspected that there will be a drop in the price of various financial assets, many market participants sell the assets to cash out because they are trying, in some way, to get back in possession of currency so that they can use it to acquire other assets.

This happens when there is any kind of crisis or when you notice that financial asset values are about to drop in value.

The result is an increase in the demand for currency, in this case clearly referring to US dollars, and it is precisely for this reason that operators or users immediately sell assets: to secure more liquidity.

People often make the mistake of not considering the US dollar or euros as financial assets, when in fact they are to all intents and purposes.

There is a whole market dedicated to the exchange of currencies which is called **Forex**.

Even Bitcoin, after all, behaves like a currency so, when we talk about dollars on the financial market, we are talking about an asset like many others with its characteristics and peculiarities but which is traded in the exact same way.

This means that the U.S. dollar is traded identically to Bitcoin or stocks, responding to the same trading rules.

In the same way that when many people want to buy Bitcoin (demand increases), it increases in value (price increases), in the same way, when many people want to acquire dollars or sell their assets, the value of the dollar also increases.

Commonly, the value of Bitcoin is considered as a dollar price, i.e., its exchange rate in dollars.

This price inevitably drops as the value of the dollar increases.

If there is therefore a demand for a dollar in the market, as mentioned above, its price or value increases in correspondence to the demand.

And this is the reason why, if the price of Bitcoin falls, often the prices of stocks fall too or vice versa, since it all depends on the fact that the reference point is the dollar that characterizes both things and that shifts their value according to the need of the moment.

This is a phenomenon that only partially explains the coincidence between Bitcoin and stocks, because it could also happen that the demand for Bitcoin or stocks increases and not for dollars.

The dynamic that causes a sudden change in the value of the U.S. dollar to affect the prices of Bitcoin and U.S. market stocks (which are both denominated in dollars) has macroscopic effects, especially when the value of the U.S. dollar varies greatly over the short term.

In fact, during periods when dollar price variability is more constant and essentially less noticeable, this dynamic does not occur.

The recent increase in the value of the dollar could then be followed by a new decline that would bring the value of the dollar back to the level it had a few weeks earlier.

It is good to expect that if this dynamic repeats itself again it could act again on the price of Bitcoin and the price of stocks traded on U.S. exchanges.

WILL BITCOIN CONSUMPTION BE ABLE TO DECREASE OVER TIME?

One of the biggest concerns regarding Bitcoin concerns its energy consumption; in fact it consumes a lot of electricity but what not everyone knows is that this consumption over the years, indeed decades, will decrease.

First of all, the consumption of Bitcoin does not come from transactions, because it is true that transactions consume energy, but it is very little.

Consumption comes mainly from mining, i.e. the so-called proof of work, the activity that must be done to validate blocks.

For each validated block, to date, 12.5 Bitcoins or more than 40,000 dollars are given away.

Receiving 40,000 dollars for each mined block means that you can invest a lot of money in electricity to mine, but in reality then the situation is more complex, because mining is a competition and only the single miner who manages to mine a block receives the prize.

It's not always the same, so you have to mine to try to eliminate many lossy blocks without succeeding before you get to mine even one.

When, at any moment, miners' revenues are halved they will be unable to do anything at all.

The only thing to do will be to reduce costs and at that point, inevitably, revenues will be cut in half and the only way to continue to make money is to reduce everything (almost 100%), especially electricity.

Simply put, if you have to suddenly cut your costs in half, all you can do is reduce your electricity consumption.

By the time the premiums run out, the miners already have a strategy that will necessarily have to go through a reduction in costs, indeed, a halving of costs.

There is also another phenomenon that affects the consumption of Bitcoin and that is the price of Bitcoin because those 12.5 Bitcoins are always the same that will become 6.25, but their value changes over time and the costs and therefore the consumption may have also increased (which is what is happening). Since halving in 2016, consumption has actually increased because the price has increased so much.

Consumption has increased because the value of Bitcoin rewards has increased and the cost has increased, as in the competition they try to invest as much as possible to eliminate as many blocks as possible.

So, if the price of Bitcoin continues to rise, the cost of mining Bitcoin could easily go back up and thus drive consumption up as well.

There are, then, two simultaneous phenomena: on the one hand, the rise in Bitcoin prices that bring a rise in costs and therefore consumption of the miner and, on the other hand, the halving of the premium and revenues of mining and therefore consequently also costs and consumption.

To date, the first phenomenon, i.e. the price increase, is preponderant and therefore Bitcoin consumption is steadily increasing for pennies, in the sense that every now and then it goes down a little, every now and then it goes up again, however the trend is one of growth.

After 2020 the price shouldn't have who knows what particular impact and may continue to grow, so consumption may continue to grow the same but in a while the premium reduction will become more significant because, at some point, the price of Bitcoin may stop growing (and thus energy consumption will increase).

Therefore, still for a few years, the consumption of Bitcoin will continue to increase but, expected a few decades, will begin to decline because mining will earn less and less and will be forced, by necessity, to reduce costs and therefore energy consumption.

Of course, consumption will never go to zero, and even when it does drop, perhaps it won't drop so drastically because that's the virtue of Bitcoin.

Mining will still be a quite profitable activity and therefore still a big consumption; until the premium will be reduced to be irrelevant and the miners will have to be satisfied with the fees, then in fact the consumption will really have to be reduced.

BITCOIN SCAMS

A good portion of those who try to learn how to make money from Bitcoin run into scams that can also be recognized due to typical workings they often make use of.

It is very easy to spot such a deception, as only a *small investment* is required in the beginning, which means giving money to a person who will maybe give some of it back and then start having *technical problems*, not being able to keep returning this money.

Some of these scammers, moreover, are part of real pyramid schemes i.e., if a person is robbed in this way, he learns the scam technique, will do it to others and recover the money he initially lost, and so on.

It will not be a way to make money, of course, but to recover, but it remains equally illicit.

These people promise earnings using words that perhaps a beginner looking for real advice doesn't understand very well and therefore believes.

On top of that, nothing they say can be easily traced to someone who is just starting out, so those who are hit with these words can't even verify what exactly they are talking about, essentially remaining in the dark about the scam they are undergoing.

To recognize these scams it is in fact important that the person in question, knows that cryptocurrencies are high risk investments and with a large margin of loss of their money. Anyone who says that you can't lose or anyone who even guarantees gains is lying and, if they are already lying at the beginning, they will most likely continue to lie.

In high-risk investments, you must enter only if you are willing to lose, so if someone invites you to invest without first making this premise, it is certainly ill-intentioned. You have to consider, at first, the investment as a loss and not as the only source of gain, but as the only source of recovery of the invested money and, only later, thanks to a little constancy, you will be able to look at the reward. There are no investments in cryptocurrencies that can be made without effort, loss and in a hurry and whoever proposes them is only and only lying to take advantage of the probable little information a beginner has.

A good teacher (if you can call him that), invites you to proceed first of all with caution in investments and therefore makes it clear that they are a great risk and can lead to the loss of money.

It could, for example, start by having its student do (again to continue the metaphor), a job that would be paid in Bitcoin.

Here again, it is good to be careful because you might be paid so little that you don't earn anything, but at least it would be a legal, though not fair, exchange.

You could go mainly at a loss perhaps for expenses, because the electricity costs are not covered by those who offered the Bitcoins but by those who use them.

In conclusion, it is good to reiterate that the fairy tale of easy, fast and effortless gain of those who try to cheat in this way is, indeed, a fairy tale.

You must therefore keep away from your investments those who make promises of this type because they will only ensure loss of money and time.

AN ECONOMIC SYSTEM BASED ON BITCOIN

Theoretically, it would be possible to create an entire economic system based on Bitcoin, i.e. instead of being based on dollars, it could work for example thanks to a marketplace in Bitcoin in which anyone puts their products or services for sale only in Bitcoin without even the exchange rate and without indicating the countervalue in dollars or dollars, but only in Bitcoin, and maybe at a fixed price.

In this way, all Bitcoins that would be traded within this economic system would always have the same value because their purchasing power (if prices in Bitcoin were fixed) would never change.

Obviously, for this to happen, Bitcoins would have to be fixed, perhaps changeable over time but not variable day to day.

Moreover, the system should not provide for the exchange of Bitcoin into fiat, i.e. people within this marketplace exchanging goods and services by buying and selling, should always do so with the same Bitcoins without ever changing them into fiat.

This way, if you have a Bitcoin, you know exactly what you can buy there with that Bitcoin and if the prices are fixed when you buy something there will be someone who receives that Bitcoin and can redeem it.

There will always be commissions to be paid to the miners but, the miners themselves, once they received those commissions, could enter this marketplace and pay back the Bitcoins they received as fees.

In other words, it would be a closed system in which always the same Bitcoins circulate without ever being exchanged into fiat currency and would have to be managed by a platform that somehow imposes fixed prices in Bitcoin and never shows fiat currency counterparts.

A platform that uses only and exclusively Bitcoin.

A system made in this way would also have a dark side, in fact, the moment you used Bitcoin with anonymous wallets to make these transactions, they would be completely obscure to the taxman, that is, it would be possible to use such a system to make profit activities completely hidden.

In fact, it is clear that such a system would actually encourage people to hide from the tax authorities because income and profit declarations are made in dollars and taxes are always paid in dollars.

Instead, when you use Bitcoin for your business, in case the value of Bitcoin goes down compared to the dollar, you would find yourself having to pay a lot more taxes than if you had used the dollar from the beginning instead.

So, the moment you use only Bitcoin and not dollars, there is an objective problem in having to pay taxes in dollars afterwards.

So much so that, nowadays, businesses accept Bitcoins and issue regular invoices and pay taxes on them in dollars, so they convert the Bitcoins received into dollars practically as soon as they receive them, otherwise they would load themselves with too much risk.

A more or less similar system is already in place, even if it is not really organized, in fact there is the **dark web** where you operate in the **dark from the tax authorities and** even from the police.

Cryptocurrencies are used here and Bitcoin is also used.

The transactions are, in some way, hidden from the IRS but also, as mentioned earlier, from law enforcement.

However, if a state decided to accept that a business using Bitcoin would prepare its accounts in Bitcoin and pay taxes in Bitcoin calculated with a percentage of Bitcoin on revenues and profits made in Bitcoin, that would be a different matter.

But we are talking about a hypothetical Bitcoin-only economic system that dispenses with fiat currencies, in which, however, businesses would have trouble paying taxes, making their own financial statements, and making profit statements in fiat currencies on the one hand, and on the other hand there would be states that would be unlikely to accept that profit-making businesses make their own financial statements, calculate taxes to be paid, and pay everything in Bitcoin.

It's pretty obvious that an economic system based only on Bitcoin could have as its main advantage and convenience precisely that of being in the dark to the taxman because otherwise there aren't actually that many advantages over using fiat money.

While it is true that a currency with a deflationary nature is better than fiat currencies in terms of savings, at the same time, it is not much of a medium of exchange for the opposite reason.

An economic system based exclusively on Bitcoin is therefore possible, however to reiterate that it would probably only really make sense if obscure to the tax authorities because otherwise it would be better to continue to use fiat currencies for economic activities and trade.

On savings, the discourse is different; in fact, a currency with a deflationary nature would certainly be better than an inflationary currency.

There is no certainty, but Bitcoin's long-term trend is indeed to increase in value, and although it is a bit early to say that this will be the case forever, the assumption is plausible.

Stablecoins would most likely play the same role as Bitcoins in this economic scenario in not paying taxes, as explained above.

To conclude, a system of trade, such as the one described, is unlikely, it is more imaginable that trade will continue to be based on inflationary currency even if the states begin to rethink their management model in terms of business based on taxes then on the forced subtraction of a part of incomes and profits.

BLOCKCHAIN

Bitcoin is based on a structure called blockchain which can be called the most difficult to solve in computing as it prevents duplication of Bitcoin or its transactions from happening.

Bitcoins can be defined as numbers or information that must not be duplicated or changed after the blockchain applies a cryptographic lock to it that only lets it display its data and not move it in any way.

The blocks are therefore encrypted and concatenated with each other, because this is precisely the characteristic of the blockchain: to be a chain of blocks with encrypted keys that cannot be changed.

Despite being impenetrable, it is spread as a public ledger that can be consulted by everyone and untouchable by those who would somehow want to attack it to modify it, because to do so would require retracing the blockchain that is displayed by everyone.

Which is very difficult to do, if not impossible.

Even if you were able to modify your own, you could not modify those of others because you would have to track all users.

Since Bitcoin was born, there have been several attempts to modify the blockchain, but they have all failed precisely because of the fact that, despite being a ledger accessible to everyone, it is an impenetrable tool.

A similar attack could target a bank, whose database servers display transactions just like those on the blockchain do but this, to the blockchain, could never happen because the blockchain system makes it very difficult to unlock them by modification.

In addition, on Bitcoin reigns the so-called peer to peer, which is a working system that sees all users as equals, so there is no one in charge of Bitcoin if not the protocol that actually does nothing but regulate it.

Each block can be analyzed and revisited in the moment of real need because precisely the blockchain is free and public and, like Bitcoin, is not subject to anything but the protocol.

You can find out all the Bitcoin transactions that are included in this block and it will be, give or take, a few thousand per transaction.

You can also find out who sent it i.e. the wallet it came from, who it came to and exactly how much money was sent.

Although you can see this wallet information, you can't see the addresses it corresponds to, or rather, you can't trace it back to who owns that wallet.

In fact, Bitcoin's blockchain provides great anonymity.

For transactions, once they are entered into blocks, you make sure that these blocks are confirmed with the cryptographic key and become irreversible.

So the blockchain makes the transactions entered into it inviolable, which is to be said an extraordinary tool since it does so independently of any gesture or person using it. Whoever uses it accepts it as it is designed and produced.

To recap, the blockchain is a chain with no dominant parties, but it poses to all users, i.e. nodes, equally.

It allows transactions to be processed, saved and protected in a very fast time (10 minutes), as this is the time in which a block is closed from time to time.

Obviously, there are other chains that use this technology that instead are very fast; for some, it even takes just a few minutes or seconds and they are also cheaper, since, to enter a transaction within a block, you pay a commission.

With other cryptocurrencies, transactions and fee costs are different but the fact that this blockchain is searchable by everyone and acts as a public ledger while being inviolable makes it unique.

It could be used in many other areas besides Bitcoins, precisely because of its essential features, such as, for example, car record management.

For example, the public stock exchange has stated that it will employ a new management system using blockchain, which is simpler and much faster and also much more secure.

The applications of blockchain are really so many, whenever you are dealing with a public ledger to put it online and make it secure, effective and powerful.

Its technology has been defined as "about to spread into many areas and change them by revolutionizing their management", precisely because it does not allow in any way its duplication.

There are those who argue that in the financial world it is, in fact, the blockchain that is disruptive, and not Bitcoin.

In truth, the blockchain makes little sense if there are no Bitcoins.

Satoshi creates this coin with the intent of regulating all the nodes that would be formed to use it as an equal.

Bitcoins are distributed according to the will of the protocol, i.e. in a consensual and identical manner for everyone.

Therefore, one can look at the blockchain as a sequential structure to whose queue new data, i.e. Bitcoin blocks, are attached.

Satoshi's invention is nothing more than digital gold, because Bitcoin is a transferable but unduplicable currency.

To get information about a Bitcoin, you have to calculate the so-called hash, which consists of the unique fingerprint of this currency.

That is why it is said that it is unique in its way.

From Bitcoins, in fact, it can be traced back in the blockchain to the origin through the different transactions that are marked and attributed to the blocks.

That fingerprint that is inserted into a Bitcoin transaction (i.e. its timestamp feature), date and time on the blockchain represents, in fact, the action of taking a physical document, putting a date and signature on it and, who will be able to guarantee the authenticity and validity of that document, will be whoever gets the win of that blockchain.

However, notarization systems like the blockchain are not essential to Bitcoin, which essentially acts like a large gold reserve for those who own them.

However, just as we have become accustomed to the presence of central banks to deal with the inflation rate and the management of the currency issued and withdrawn from the market, in the same way we can become accustomed to new currencies being used as reserve assets that can achieve the price stability of monetary theory, according to which a currency must be as stable as a linear meter in order not to cause losses or too many gains.

But that would be kind of like if the roads got longer and shorter and everyone went and re-measured the roads to make them all the same again.

However, this is exactly what happens to currency when prices change: it has to be reestablished by someone, i.e. the banks that regulate taxes on it.

That's why you can't look at Bitcoin as trivially similar to a physical currency, because it has savings, or reserve, capabilities that make it not superficial at all but a source of income that is by the way well distributed and not private.

In fact, Bitcoin can be said to be a champion in its field because it has a large group of users around the world and an elastic monetary policy but, more importantly, it was not a martyr of the era of digitization of currency and has survived until today.

While so many coins with the same asset type didn't even finish being put on the market that they went out.

LIGHTING NETWORK

The lighting network is a Bitcoin software.

To understand how it works you have to start with the Bitcoin blockchain.

This has two problems: it's slow and it's expensive.

It consists of a blockchain where a new block is added every 10 minutes. So, when you make a Bitcoin transaction, you have to wait for at least 10 minutes.

Moreover, if at any given time there are a lot of transactions waiting to be placed in a new block, since they stay there, there is always a risk that a transaction will be left out of the blocks.

Gradually it catches up with the blockchain but there is a long wait.

Typically, to try to make sure you get into the first block, you have to pay some pretty hefty fees.

While they're not actually particularly high now, during the peak in 2017 you had to spend as much as $15-20 to make sure you could get a transaction onto the block immediately.

With lighting network, instead, transactions are immediate and cost a few thousandths of a dollar; in fact in this way transactions do not pass through the blockchain and that's why they can be not slow and not expensive.

In order to use lighting network to send/receive Bitcoin, you will have to open a channel.

The opening is a transaction and then all transactions that follow take place off chain (not on the blockchain) and are directed by the stakeholders and then, when the channel is closed (assuming one wants to close it), a second transaction will be made.

There are only two transactions that pass through the blockchain: the one to open the channel and the eventual one to close the channel, while all the others are direct between the sender and the receiver.

These go through nodes, so they are very fast and economical.

It's called Bitcoin's second layer because it's a second layer, a separate system but based on Bitcoin's blockchain.

It works perfectly with Bitcoin in an alternative way, plus it is a p2p (**peer to peer**) network. It is decentralized and does not involve having to hand over custody of your funds to someone else.

There are now more than 6,000 lighting networks because they have, in fact, many advantages over traditional transactions: they are virtually immediate and at very low cost, so low that you can even make **microtransactions** lighting network of 20 cents of a dollar.

Through traditional services (like paypal) it could be a problem, because the transaction costs could be more than 20 cents, instead with lighting network sending an equivalent of 20 cents will cost about 2-4 thousandths, so totally irrelevant.

Benefits of the lighting network:

- It enables Bitcoin scalability by avoiding the 10-minute wait thanks to numerous nodes that can support the significant increase in transaction volume, without interfering with the blockchain.

- Total anonymity is guaranteed as transactions on the blockchain are marked, while on the lighting network they are not.

So publicly you will only see the opening and closing of the channel.

The **limitations**, however, of lighting network are that only Bitcoins can be used on the channel and that once the teamwork begins and a certain amount of Bitcoins is introduced, only that amount can be used.

So the only way to take back the used Bitcoins is to close the channel and send them back to a traditional wallet.

It is better to put on a lighting network channel only the Bitcoins you want to spend and keep aside those you want to keep in the long run.

It is a secure technology that is, however, not yet widespread and widely used.

Moreover, then the teamnetwork allows other developments in addition to the uses listed above.

For example, develop the so-called lighting applications which are nothing but the apps made for lighting network very interesting.

It would be perfect for e-commerce sites, especially those that sell low or very low cost products, precisely because it would virtually eliminate commissions.

It is good to remember that, in the transitions, the commissions are paid by those who send the Bitcoins so, for example, in the case of an e-commerce site, the commissions, if it used the lighting network would not be paid by the site but by the customer and for the customer to add 2-3 or 4 thousandths of a dollar to make the transaction is relatively very little.

For example, they are considering integrating lighting network on twitter to make micro donations of even a penny.

There are already 6,000 nodes and more than 10,000 channels lighting network because this network is spreading very fast, so much so that in the future it can become an excellent system of exchange of values in Bitcoin.

It still remains a deflationary currency, so probably not extraordinary as a transactional currency, but perhaps great as a store of value.

As for fiat currencies, it must be said that they are and continue to be excellent transactional coins, if they are used as tokens, that is in the form of stable coin, they are really extraordinary.

PEER TO PEER

Peer to peer stands for a non-hierarchical computer network, that is, in which all nodes are equal.

An example of what is a hierarchical system is a soccer team in which there are the players, the goalkeeper, the coach, and finally the corporate investors who manage the finances.

The members are subject to each other because there are those who make the decisions and there are those who must execute them, and each has a role that is different from the others.

In a peer network, there is no hierarchy, so everyone has the same role and performs the same activity (which is very difficult to imagine within a soccer team, of course).

The members of the network at par are the nodes that have, in fact, all the same work to do. No one among them can take decisions on the other because their power, of vote and action, is exactly equal to that of the others.

They are all accountable to the IT protocol that says what network members and nodes can do.

In all likelihood, this is the most democratic IT architecture of all, since it has an equal internal structure, the operating principle of which is the established IT protocol.

The latter acts as a textbook of rules and duties in order to be part of the network.

This protocol must be strictly adhered to otherwise you risk non-admission to a node.

The two big advantages of this network are the lack of a hierarchy that imposes absurd powers among peers (in fact we can say that it is a democratic informatic structure) and the other advantage is the concept of perfect respect of the protocol that is at the base of p2p networks. Moreover protocols are public and anyone can verify what that protocol does or how it is made in order to use it.

In fact, you have to strictly respect it.

There is, in fact, no concept of trust within the network thanks to the presence of the protocol that guarantees the invariability of these rules.

The networks in question are said to be "decentralized" because they do not have a command center and do not have a hierarchy with a leader.

They can be defined "trustless" because there is no trust principle in the use of the network, but you depend only and solely on the protocol of it and not on others.

In fact it's a revolutionary system that could be easily extended to the payment system, since nobody could be manipulated or nobody could miss anything of the regulation, since if you don't respect it you are simply excluded from the network.

So, in a nutshell, the two things that set the network apart are **decentralization** and **trustlessness**.

Even the internet itself is decentralized, as it was created at a time when the US wanted a network that could withstand even nuclear power and, therefore, unassailable or undisturbed by third parties.

Peer to peer can be considered an evolution of the internet that continues to function even if some members do not respect the rules, precisely because they are no longer included in its mechanisms.

TOKEN

The term *token,* brings back a bit 'to the environment of American casinos, where they are often used as coins or resemble their physical appearance.

To understand tokens (which relate to cryptocurrencies), you have to imagine those mentioned before but in a digital form, becoming just computer information.

The tokens represent, in fact, the coins of which cryptocurrencies are made up.

There are two types of cryptocurrency tokens: historical ones, such as Bitcoin, which we refer to very little and today's tokens that represent digital currency.

This distinction is even made by the Swiss state agency for financial market supervision.

In fact, they are distinguished precisely by the categories in which they function, i.e. trade exchange and investment respectively.

There is a difference between coin tokens and coins which are trivially cryptocurrencies that have their own ledger and a blockchain, so like Bitcoin.

On the other hand, when someone creates tokens using the Ethereum blockchain but that are not eternal and there are new types of tokens, these are called, precisely, *tokens* which is their most popular definition.

Cryptocurrencies can be said to have a completely separate life from tokens that do not possess a registry, blockchain or otherwise operating protocol.

Whereas instead they are probably closer to a coin like token that has all these features like Bitcoin.

Many of the coins that are minted and distributed on the digital market are nothing more than tokens and they move thanks to smart contracts that facilitate their exchange into other currencies.

So, it is good to reiterate that the operation of the coins without standard protocols that are new and do not have a backing of this type, are easily erasable and nothing to do with the tokens of second definition that is their own coin with blockchain and the rest.

FORKS

You have to imagine that the blockchain of a currency is a chain because, precisely, it means chain of blocks.

This, at some point, may split into a bifurcation and thus create a second chain.

These chains, in reality, are not physical but are computer-based and are generated thanks to a computer protocol that regulates how they are to be constituted.

For the bifurcation to occur, what happens is that a **new** protocol is introduced to the old one that follows its own **new instructions**.

While the old block with their own protocol continue on their way.

The two chains, by necessity, cannot remain united because Bitcoin only works if the whole network follows the same protocol, and if this is changed, then these secondary chains are born, united only up to the last block of the blockchain that had been the same for both.

For example, as of 1August 2017, a second chain, also of Bitcoin, but with a new protocol, was created and then forked again.

In fact, when the two chains separate, the tokens that were on the old one duplicate on the beginning of the new one, the latter then proceeds independently from the old one.

But the fact that there is this doubling, does not imply that the value of the tokens, therefore of the Bitcoins in question, is doubled.

They are simply copied to give history to the chain.

After a protocol change, the tokens will be different because they are subject to a different protocol, so in order to use them you will have to use another wallet, different from the original one of the chain to which the tokens belonged before.

THE TETHER DOLLAR (USDT)

On the financial markets, Bitcoin is mostly traded in **US dollars.**

So, most of the Bitcoin purchases that are made in the market are made with dollars.

The latter is not a cryptocurrency, but is like fiat currencies with all the limitations that come with it; in particular, there are three major limitations in using the US dollar:

- Not in all countries of the world is it possible to use the American dollar.

If you have a bank account in a foreign country, it is difficult to have, send or receive dollars precisely because some countries do not allow their use;

- Transactions in U.S. dollars are restricted by banks.

If a transaction is suspicious to the bank, it is stopped, blocked, and monitored;

- U.S. dollars are not anonymous; when they are used from a card or bank account there is always the possibility that those in charge can see the identity of the owner and, therefore, understand how he is using them.

Cryptocurrencies, on the other hand, do not suffer from these limitations as they can be used all over the world; there is no limit or control over the transactions that you make and they can be used completely anonymously.

It was devised (to solve all the limitations listed above), a cryptocurrency that would follow, verbatim, the value of the U.S. dollar; this was called **USDT** and was issued by **Tether**, but is also commonly called crypto dollar.

It works in a seemingly trivial way since, if you want to buy 1 USDT you have to pay 1$, and vice versa as far as selling is concerned.

All this is done through an Exchange called **Bit Phoenix** that belongs to the same group of companies as Tether, which provides the tokens that will then be exchanged on the Exchange site.

Tether does not have its own blockchain but relies on **Ethereum's**, so the vast majority of USDT in circulation are tokens issued on the Ethereum network that require, (to be moved), to pay transaction fees in Ethereum and TH.

If you view Market's site, you can see which exchange pairs on the markets are most commonly used involving Bitcoin.

First is Bitcoin - tether on Binance, second is Bitcoin - tether on OKEx and only in third place is Bitcoin - USDT on Coinbase Pro and finally, in fourth position, Bitcoin - USDT on HtBTC.

This means that, nowadays, most of the Bitcoins that are traded on the market, are no longer traded in US dollars but in USDT because those in the industry prefer it since they do not have to stay within the limits that were listed above.

So you can easily exchange USDT with other currencies but you cannot exchange US dollars in the same way.

Besides, Tether guarantees a certain degree of anonymity if it is used in the appropriate way and in the most appropriate places.

It can be clearly stated that Tether has become the replacement for the US dollar within the crypto world, because it maintains this value over time and because it is practically always traded and used as if it were $1 but with the advantages that are granted to tokens.

This preference, in fact, as seen in the rankings, is increasingly expanding due to its convenience.

However, you need to pay particular attention to two points:

- The USDT does not necessarily remain at parity with the US dollar forever; if those selling them were to experience issues, parity could be lost and at that point USDT token holders would lose value because the token would have decreased in value.

Tether claims that 100% of USDT tokens are backed by funds: roughly with 75% of them, by as many USDT tokens and with 25% backed by other assets.

There is no proof of these statements but no one has had any problems to date because the service provided has been fully functional.

- Let us now consider stablecoins such as the USDT.

Their value (even if there was a huge growth in USDT usage), would remain the same as $1.

Since the dollar is an inflationary currency, if it were to lose value so would the USDT but always aligning with the dollar.

In May 2021 an article was published on Business Insider Italy where it discusses how at that time neither Bitcoin nor paypal were the most used digital payment systems in the world, but Tether was.

In fact, the total number of transactions in those days had far exceeded that of Bitcoin and paypal.

Despite this, Bitcoin remains at the top of the leaderboard by sum of the value of transactions executed, though not by the number of them.

Stablecoins, in all likelihood, will be increasingly used due to their stable value and the fact that they are a great alternative to fiat currencies precisely because they have no limitations, but especially because transactions can be done anonymously.

CRYPTOCURRENCY EXCHANGE

In order to use American dollars in stores where another currency is used, such as the euro (for example), you will have to try to change the dollars into euros.

To do this, you can turn to a money changer, that is, someone who has euros and is willing to agree to give you your euros in exchange for dollars.

The exchange takes place at market price, and usually the money changer charges a commission (which is his profit).

In the opposite case, euro to dollar, you go to the money changer and they should have these dollars. In the case of changing to some slightly more exotic and hard-to-find currency, (which is maybe the Philippine peso), the money changer may not have this exact money.

The problem is solved online, because online platforms work all over the world.

These cryptocurrency exchange platforms are called **Exchanges and are** used to exchange cryptocurrencies for other currencies or fiat currencies.

Currency Exchanges work very similar to traditional exchanges but with some differences: the main one is that when you go on the Exchange and want to change your cryptocurrencies into others, it acts as a marketplace, where anyone can put their cryptocurrencies or fiat currencies up for sale and exchange them for others.

In other words, an Exchange site is very similar to a stock exchange where there are people buying and people selling.

For example:

> You have Bitcoins and you want to convert them to dollars, so you go to an Exchange that accepts both Bitcoins and dollars (since it is not obvious since there are many that do not accept dollars), you load the Bitcoins and put them on sale at the price you want or at the market price at that moment.
>
> If there is someone willing to buy Bitcoins by giving dollars in exchange, then the exchange will happen and in this way you will have exchanged Bitcoins for someone else's dollars.

On the Exchange these exchanges are managed in a totally automatic way; you don't know who is giving the dollars, everything is done directly by the platform that looks for buyers or sellers interested in exchanging the currency you want to exchange what you are selling.

So, if you put Bitcoin up for sale because you want to exchange it into dollars, the platform will look for someone who is willing to buy Bitcoins paying in dollars at that moment.

But this applies to any type of exchange pair, for example if the exchange pair is Bitcoin and tether it means that you can put Bitcoin or tether up for sale and receive tether or Bitcoin in return respectively.

Obviously, as well as the cash registers of money changers, the Exchange keeps a small percentage, often very low definitely less than that of traditional money changers.

There are even some exchanges that do not have commissions at the moment, but they are few and very limited, moreover these platforms are real marketplaces, since you can choose the price yourself.

Once you have found who wants to buy what you have put up for sale, the so-called deal happens, or rather, the trade specifically.

If instead the price is too high maybe there is nobody in that moment who wants to buy and therefore no trade takes place.

If you are in a hurry, you can not put any price and let the platform make the price, (of course it will be lower).

However, Exchanges are not only used to exchange currencies, but are also used for trading because you can also earn money with currency exchanges.

If you put Bitcoins up for sale when their value in dollars is high and cash out dollars, then maybe you can use those dollars to buy back Bitcoins when the price is low.

Doing so generates surplus value and therefore profit.

In fact there are people who do this professionally, they are in fact professional traders who do business on Exchange sites.

You have to pay attention to a couple of peculiarities:

- Each Exchange has its own prices, i.e. if you put Bitcoins up for sale on one Exchange at one price, it is not certain that they will also sell at the same price on another Exchange, because each one is its own market, so it will have different prices.

- Not all Exchanges have the same currencies, there are some that have a few currencies some that have many, some that only have cryptocurrencies some that also have fiat currencies.

Before trading on the Exchanges, it's a good idea to find out what currencies are supported; almost all cryptocurrencies can be traded in Bitcoin, or however the vast majority can also be traded in tether dollars.

Exchanges that also support fiat currencies such as dollar and euro have stricter requirements and therefore not all of them accept to support them, so there are not so many Exchanges that allow to trade fiat currencies as well.

Often, to buy a minor cryptocurrency, one must first convert the fiat currency to Bitcoin and then afterwards use Bitcoin to buy these minor cryptocurrencies.

Since Exchanges are private sites, it is advisable never to leave assets or funds in the wallets of Exchanges because, if by chance that Exchange is hacked or fails, you risk losing all your funds.

In fact, after making exchanges, it is a good idea to transfer the currency obtained to a private wallet where it can be recovered as many times as you want.

IS IT POSSIBLE TO PRINT MORE MONEY?

Usually when something seems too good to be true, it is false, again, **printing money or minting money** to try to solve problems is basically an **ineffective solution**, even dangerous.

But first of all it is necessary to specify well what it means to print money:

> In fact, most of the coins that are used are not in paper format; the bulk of them are in electronic, or digital, format.
>
> When you use the definition of "printing money" you are referring to something else, namely the creation of money out of nothing, in this case dollars, especially in digital format.
>
> Coins like the euro or dollar, like all modern currencies, are called fiat currencies because they don't have anything underlying them.
>
> In a few words, they don't have value because they represent something of value, but they have value only because they are used by citizens, companies and states to make exchanges, so since they don't represent an underlying and they don't represent something of value, they can be created virtually in infinite quantity.

The **value** that is **written** on the 500 dollar bill is actually totally arbitrary and means nothing.

The only thing that has meaning is that if a banknote has that particular number written on it, that banknote will have a **face value** that will always be 500 dollars never 501 and never 499.

But the so called nominal value of currency is totally arbitrary, actually the real value of currency is its **purchasing power**, that is how many things you can buy with that 500 dollars.

For example, in Italy before 2001, you could buy very few things with 100 liras, with 100 Euros today you can buy much more.

This is not because the lira was worth less than the dollar, but because the face value of the banknotes, i.e. the face value of 100 lira, doesn't really mean anything.

Just as the nominal value of 100 dollars does not really mean anything, what counts is the purchasing power of the total amount of money you have.

Purchasing power **is not fixed**, but **varies over time**, so if the face value of a banknote remains the same, its purchasing power varies and usually decreases because prices increase.

Prices always tend to increase over time, so the more prices in the market increase, the fewer things I can buy with that currency.

Therefore, the purchasing power of one's own money decreases as the prices of the things one can buy increase.

One could ask: "*why not create a lot of money out of nothing and distribute it to citizens since technically it could be done, precisely because the purchasing power of money varies over time and if there is too much money on the market it devalues and loses purchasing power causing prices to rise too much?*"

Make this assumption:

> The state decides to print another 1,000 dollars out of thin air, in addition to those you own, and give them to a person as a gift.
>
> Therefore in that case it would not have more 1000 dollar to spend but 2.000 dollar.
>
> The most probable thing is that the individual begins to spend even more, but the products to buy on the market would be the same, because printing money increases production, it simply increases the liquidity available to those who want to buy those products.
>
> So it would increase the number of people who want to buy the products but the products would remain the same and this would inevitably increase the price of these products, because the price of products is precisely the relationship between supply and demand.
>
> If demand goes up and supply doesn't, the price inevitably goes up as well.

So creating money out of nothing and distribute it to citizens only serves to make them increase spending, further increasing prices and therefore affecting the purchasing power of money.

Eventually, you get back to exactly where you were before.

It could be proposed that a law would mandate that prices cannot be raised.

This is not possible, however, for the simple reason that prices cannot be set by law, but must be set by the market.

From the moment a price is imposed by law, which is perhaps lower than the market price, the products disappear from the regulated market and reappear in the **black market**, illegal, where these laws imposing prices would not be respected.

So, imposing prices by law, means to make the goods escape and go to the unregulated black market where they have their real price or even higher than they would have on the regulated market in case there were no prices set by law.

This has already happened in the past; many countries throughout history have created money and distributed it to their citizens, triggering inflationary or even hyperinflationary processes.

> In countries such as Venezuela where inflation was at staggering levels and prices were rising day by day, so it was better to buy in the morning than in the evening because in the morning the goods cost less and in the evening they cost more.
>
> In states like Zimbabwe, which hyperinflated the currency so much, they had to eliminate it.
>
> In fact, the Zimbabwe dollar no longer exists because it had devalued so much that it was no longer worth anything.

So, yes, it is possible to create money out of nothing and distribute it to citizens, but not only is it useless but it also risks generating more harm than good, as for example happened in Venezuela or Zimbabwe.

If on the other hand this operation of creating money out of nothing and distributing it to citizens is done once and with moderation as the US is doing, where they are creating money and distributing it to citizens to cope with the emergency, in that case the price increase will most likely occur but will be contained.

At this stage, prices are rising too little because inflation has been below the 2% target for quite some time, so creating money and distributing it to citizens, paradoxically can lead to some advantage.

Citizens have more money to spend, it is true that this will increase prices, but at this moment an increase in prices for example in the USA is not a particularly bad thing.

If the money created was not distributed to citizens, it would not reach the consumer markets, but would be retained for example by the financial markets, as happened after the crisis of 2008 and 2009: both the American central bank and the European central bank, but in fact also the Bank of Japan and the Bank of England, created and placed on the financial markets large amounts of money that however remained there and did not go to citizens.

Therefore, they have not entered the circuit of consumer markets and therefore have not inflated the prices of essential goods.

They have, however, **inflated financial asset prices**.

The important aspect of printing more money is to do so with moderation, to avoid triggering inflationary spirals that cause prices to rise too much, making people lose purchasing power, especially those with savings and fixed salaries.

The **main victims** of such a process would be **pensioners** because their pension, and the amount of money they would receive, would continue to be the same but would be worth less as they would have less purchasing power.

If today we wanted to print money, to create money to solve problems, we would have to increase the rate at which new money is already created and this could be a serious risk because it could trigger inflationary spirals, even hyperinflationary, so we must be careful.

Coins like Bitcoin, on the other hand, cannot be created at will, i.e. Bitcoin cannot be issued indefinitely while instead there is no **theoretical cap** on how many euros to how many dollars can be created and put on the market.

This cap is not only theoretical but also practical and concrete as a maximum of 21 million Bitcoins can be created.

Currently, more than 18 million have already been created so we are almost at the maximum number of Bitcoins that can enter circulation.

This is because the whole thing is based on an open source computer protocol, virtually public and not modifiable, which then establishes once and for all that at most there will be 21 million Bitcoins in circulation.

So, while traditional fiat currencies are inflationary because they are created in large quantities in order to generate a price inflation of about 2% per year, instead Bitcoin is said to have a deflationary nature, that is, it has a path that goes towards the opposite, that is, towards the non-action of new Bitcoins in order to ensure that its purchasing power instead increases over time instead of reducing as inevitably happens with fiat currencies.

Therefore, not only printing money to solve all the problems does not work, but even exaggerating with the printing of money creates even more problems so it is essential to do it with moderation and being careful not to generate inflationary or even hyperinflationary spirals that could harm the population.

INFLATION AND DEFLATION

Inflation and deflation are economic and financial concepts related to price trends and the value of money. They are the opposite of each other.

Inflation is a prolonged increase in the general average price level over a given period of time, usually over the course of a year, which generates a decrease in the purchasing power of money.

For inflation, in fact, happens what is the fear of anyone who has savings in the bank, in fact, for example, 100 dollars are always 100 dollars, but as a result of a process of inflation will not change their value, rather will change their purchasing power, or what you can buy with that 100 after they have lost value and prices have increased.

The same reasoning, unfortunately, applies to pensions, which always remain fixed over time, but their value is given by the currency which can suffer a great loss of purchasing power due to inflation.

Inflation has advantages and disadvantages, especially if it is not filled or controlled during the course of the year, it could create great inconvenience.

The advantage that could be enjoyed during a period of inflation is that whoever collects money, in spite of his loss of purchasing power, also collects a lot of it because prices have also been increased.

This could further come in handy if you have to pay off a debt.

It is true that the nominal value of it would always remain the same, but the money that would be spent to pay it back would be worth less.

Inflation could be called advantageous because it tends to keep people from waiting in the process of making purchases because the price could rise further.

As for deflation, which is the opposite of inflation, again there are disadvantages and advantages.

As for the example of debt, with deflation it becomes a problem because just as when there is inflation, the value of real debt decreases, in deflation the value of real debt increases, meaning it becomes more difficult to pay.

Deflation involves a decrease in prices, but it is not advisable to make purchases immediately; rather it is better to wait for them to decrease and then buy at an even lower price.

This factor can be said to not make deflation precisely the favorite of modern economies.

One advantage certainly is on savings because if you have money set aside and there is deflation, the value of that money increases over time.

The same reasoning applies to those with fixed incomes (such as pensions), because they can buy everything they need and more at a much lower price.

These are two great extremes, but following a middle ground in which you exclude both would not be good, as the debt problem is crucial so usually the optimal situation is considered to be inflation at around 2%.

In this way, prices increase slightly and there is time to adjust salaries, but at the same time the total debt also decreases by 2% per year, which is not a bad thing at all for consumption.

While deflation is good for savings, this makes it so that nowadays there are inflationary currencies more suitable for trade and deflationary ones made for savings.

Often the cause of inflation is precisely fiat currency, which can be distributed without limit by central banks to its citizens.

Obviously these do not distribute inappropriately for the 2% inflation ceiling that must be sustained but not exceeded.

Another thing that can increase inflation is an increase in earnings, therefore incomes. Because the more you earn, the more you spend, the more prices rise.

And it is precisely for this reason that deflationary coins, such as Bitcoin, were born, whose distribution does not actually increase over time, but several of these coins disappear from circulation after a while, leaving room for the introduction of new ones.

As already explained, the number of Bitcoins in circulation will decrease to a standstill, but the number of dollars in circulation will do the exact opposite by increasing, precisely because the central bank of Europe wants to keep the inflation rate steady at 2% no matter what happens.

To recap, fiat currencies are inflationary and are so precisely because they are issued by a bank that has every interest in them being so.

They are also ideal currencies for trade and encourage consumer markets.

In contrast, deflationary coins are limited in number and distribution and are ideal for savings.

These change their price very easily because they are precisely characterized by volatility.

IT'S TRUE THAT GOLD DOESN'T ALWAYS BEAT INFLATION

Gold is considered the good of refuge par excellence, because it is said that in the course of time it never loses its value, but if you go to check the calculation of the variation of the value of gold over time, that is, the years or decades, you find that for example it is known that due to inflation, the traditional fiat currencies such as the euro or the dollar, lose value because they lose purchasing power.

The question that arises is "*what to do if something similar happens to gold?*", that is, to ask how the purchasing power of gold varies over the years, or rather its true value. In other words: does gold beat inflation over time or not?

> There is a study that reveals the following between 1979 and 2017, so basically over the last 40 years, and looking at the five-year cycles, i.e. from five years to five years gold outperformed inflation only in 45% of the cases, i.e. more than half of the five-year cycle between the year 1979 and 2017.
>
> The value of gold has increased less than inflation.
>
> In other words, it is not true that gold never loses its value, but it is true that every now and then it increases and every now and then it decreases, even in relation to inflation, and what counts therefore is the average over time.

When the price of gold rises, it becomes more profitable to produce it, that is to extract it, so when the price of gold increases, then tends to increase the production and marketing.

Therefore, if the price of gold rises then, as a consequence, the scarcity is reduced and this tends then in the long run to lead to a fall in the price of gold and so to speak a sustained increase in production.

If you look at a chart that shows the price of gold net of inflation, you can see that at certain times, the price of gold goes very high but then afterwards it tends to go down, precisely because when there are these spikes they probably cause an increase in production.

This increase in production later encourages the price of gold to fall.

This chart works like this:

> It takes as its reference value 1, in April 1968, and then calculates what the growth rate was until April 2000.
>
> So in the course of 32 years the price of gold net of inflation has only increased by about 50%.
>
> So just over 1% per year over time.

Then from there a new uphill race was triggered that brought it back very high and was followed by a new downhill, probably after the crisis between 2008 and 2009.

Now it is growing again however it is to be expected that if it grows so much again, it can go down again in the way we have seen from the chart.

The price of gold does not go up every year more than inflation; there are periods lasting several years when it goes up much more than inflation, but there are periods just as there are times when it goes down.

This is a mechanism that goes on continuously, so there is a growth trend that, however, if spread over several years, is very limited.

This cannot happen with Bitcoin because Bitcoin production (although it would be more correct to call it Bitcoin mining) does not vary.

When the peak varies, it is worth more but no more Bitcoins are produced.

Bitcoin mining is independent of price because it is created by computer protocol that is virtually unchangeable and stipulates that a certain specific amount is created every 10 minutes and that's it.

It only varies once every four years when the inflation rate is halved on it.

So if gold when it rises in price, somehow encourages an increase in production, i.e. mining, which drives the price down, this dynamic with Bitcoin is not possible because Bitcoin mining is fixed and simply every four years it halves.

In other words, Bitcoin was designed to better guard against inflation than gold, which was not designed but mined and, later, put on the market.

Bitcoin, on the other hand, was designed and made on purpose to be more resistant to inflation than gold is.

In the nearly eleven years of Bitcoin's existence, this has already shown that in fact its growth in value over time is well above the average growth of gold.

This doesn't necessarily mean that it will go on like this, however, since there is a design behind Bitcoin that makes it potentially an even better equipped resource than gold to withstand inflation, it makes it conceivable that in theory this struggle of Bitcoin with inflation over time could also continue to be better than that of gold.

Bitcoin's scarcity index i.e. the ratio of stocks to production will become more or less similar to that of gold around 2024.

According to this report regarding Bitcoin, it will become much rarer than gold.

The reasoning in question concerns only the supply side of the market, but then the price is made not only by supply but also by demand, so for all this to cause an increase in price, and therefore the increase in the value of Bitcoin, it would be necessary that on the other side the market demand at least remained constant or increased.

If, on the other hand, the demand for Bitcoin in the market over the next few years, or decades, remains constant or increases, then Bitcoin should really resist inflation even better than gold.

DEFEND YOURSELF FROM INFLATION WITH BITCOIN

Inflation is defined as a sustained increase in the general average price level, so inflation means an increase in prices.

The consequence of rising prices is the loss of purchasing power of money.

Remember the example of bank savings, which lose purchasing power even though their nominal value is always the same.

In other words, the more prices rise, the less purchasing power the currency has.

Often this is a direct consequence of the devaluation of a currency, and the devaluation occurs at the hands of central banks, which end up decreasing the value of the currency by simply distributing too much of it.

The eventual solution that sees Bitcoin as the protagonist makes one consider multiple factors. First, this is a currency created to be decentralized and therefore does not have a bank that can produce more of it than is the limit and end up devaluing it.

In fact, it is Bitcoin's computer protocol that decides a quantity, and that quantity is indisputable until no more are issued.

Bitcoin is not an inflationary currency and does not devalue (as mentioned above).

While there is no absolute certainty that this will always happen, there is a good chance as the history of Bitcoin's average values seems to confirm a price level that is always rising considerably.

Bitcoin is also issued solely and exclusively as the protocol decides, so you can't speculate on its issuance, as the value is mutable only by the protocol.

Exactly the opposite happens, however, with central banks that can decide, in order to keep inflation at 2%, to devalue the currency by issuing too much of it.

Of course, it is all to be seen and it is good to remember that the behavior of the price of Bitcoin cannot be predicted but can only be assumed.

Thus, as far as savings or fixed incomes are concerned, these would be best arbitrarily converted into fiat currency during periods of high inflation, to avoid loss of purchasing power.

CONCLUSIONS

Trading is an opportunity for anyone who wants to create an extra-work income or for those who even want to quit their job and do this activity full time.

The choice of the right strategy must be made consciously by the person on the basis of his emotions and on the basis of his attitude to risk.

This is the only way to be profitable in the long run.

The global knowledge is essential, but then the difference between a winning and a losing trader is made by the strategy and the head.

Don't try to overdo it in trying to prove you're a visionary or trying to beat the market.

If you have this kind of approach you will only lose money.

Set yourself short, medium and long term goals, establish a plan and never deviate from it for any reason in the world. Good luck!

www.ingramcontent.com/pod-product-compliance
Lightning Source LLC
LaVergne TN
LVHW022114200926
848481LV00003B/1168
* 9 7 9 8 2 1 5 4 9 4 3 8 7 *